Your Colors At Home

Dramatic contrast for a Winter, this all black-and-white scheme updates a traditional interior. Any of your deep colors would be just as effective — royal purple, for one.

The space is contemporary ... the furnishings are traditional ...
the combination is exciting in this open-plan living/dining room.
A good setting for a Winter who enjoys her antiques, the eclectic
arrangement includes Chippendale-style dark mahogany dining
furniture and silvered mirror, formal button-tufted sofas, armless
upholstered chairs and a glass and chrome coffee table. In keeping
with the soaring scale of the room, such accessories as the
Oriental screen and plants are out-sized and dramatic.

Your Colors At Home

Decorating with Your Seasonal Colors

Lauren Smith & Rose Bennett Gilbert

Designed by Robert Hickey

ACROPOLIS BOOKS LTD.

WASHINGTON, D.C.

DEDICATION

This book is dedicated to the belief
that your home can be beautiful and colorful
no matter what your season.

 Every effort has been made to provide accurate color in the color section of this book. Owing to the limitations of the four-color printing process, however, certain discrepancies are inevitable. Therefore, the color samples in this book should be used only as a guideline.

ACROPOLIS BOOKS, LTD.
Alphons J. Hackl, Publisher
Colortone Building, 2400 17th St., N.W.
Washington, D.C. 20009

Printed in the United States of America by
COLORTONE PRESS
Creative Graphics, Inc.
Washington, D.C. 20009

Attention: Schools and Corporations
ACROPOLIS books are available at quantity discounts with bulk purchase for educational, business, or sales promotional use. For information, please write to: SPECIAL SALES DEPARTMENT, ACROPOLIS BOOKS LTD., 2400 17th ST., N.W., WASHINGTON, D.C. 20009

Are there Acropolis Books you want but cannot find in your local stores?
You can get any Acropolis book title in print. Simply send title and retail price, plus $1.00 per copy to cover mailing and handling costs for each book desired. District of Columbia residents add applicable sales tax. Enclose check or money order only, no cash please, to:
ACROPOLIS BOOKS LTD.,
2400 17th St., N.W.,
WASHINGTON, D.C. 20009.

Library of Congress Cataloging-in-Publication Data
Smith, Lauren.
  Your colors at home.
  1. Color in interior decoration. I. Gilbert,
Rose Bennett. II. Title.
NK2115.5.C6S65 1985 747'.94   85-15112
ISBN 0-87491-748-4

Your Colors at Home was designed by Robert Hickey, Art Director, and Chris Borges, Assistant Art Director. Tom Smoak and Mary Kay Carter, Artists.

WITH SPECIAL APPRECIATION

. . . From Lauren Smith to Rose Gilbert for her initial encouragement, and to Bob Smith for his total support. To Minor Bishop, Ray Kindell, and Ward Truesdale for helping me with my clients; to Jacky Sheridan for her good advice and counsel; and to Al Hackl, John Hackl, Sandy Trupp, and Dan Wallace, and all the other people at Acropolis, and especially to Valerie Avedon, Chris Borges, Robert Hickey, and Lisa Shenkle for holding *my* hand.

. . . From Rose Gilbert to Jean Green, who watched it happen, and to Aaron, Scott, and Bennett, who thought it never would.

...From both of us to Andrea Fuller, Melody Jaisson, Karen Jamison, Deborah Jennings, and Mary Shellum for their enthusiasm.

A welcome retreat for any Autumn, this sunlit study is warm with woods and leathers, and rich with hearty textures: the paneled wall, brass-studded leather trunk, and sculptured wall-to-wall carpet. In its quiet way, the carpet adds to the visual interest of the room without demanding undue attention. It also stretches space in the small area, and helps keep the peace and quiet.

CONTENTS

(handwritten annotations: 20, 31, 35)

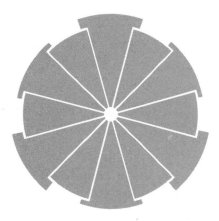

―――――――――――――――――

Lauren Smith is a practicing interior designer and color consultant to the home furnishings industry, and president of Lauren Smith, Inc., in New York City. She is a member of the American Society of Interior Designers, the Fashion Group, and the Color Marketing Group. She lives in Connecticut.

Rose Bennett Gilbert is a well-known writer and editor and has collaborated on several decorating books. She is a member and former officer of the National Home Fashions League and writes for top publications in the home fashions field. She lives in New Jersey.

INTRODUCTION

The Seasonal Color Theory Works for Rooms, Too

The theory that every one of us belongs in a general color category, or "season," is easy to understand and easier to apply, both to the clothes we wear and to the furnishings we surround ourselves with at home.

In essence, the seasonal color theory maintains that each of us is born with a certain skin coloring that can be categorized as one of four "seasons." You are either a *Winter, Summer, Autumn,* or *Spring,* and your season will never change, even with a suntan.

Once you determine your season and start to wear *your colors,* a number of delightful things begin to happen. First of all, you'll be receiving many compliments on how *you* look. *You,* not your clothes and not your makeup, although it is the total package that produces this attractive new look you are enjoying.

The natural outgrowth of this positive reinforcement is new self-confidence and a sense of *personal style.* Eventually, everything in your closet will be "in season," so getting dressed every day will become, as the psychologists put it, an "approach-approach" situation: you really can't go wrong. Clothes shopping itself will be simplified as you find yourself bypassing everything else in the store and automatically heading straight for *your colors.*

The next step is almost as automatic. You will quickly begin to gravitate to *your colors* in other areas of your life. You'll shop for a new car with *your colors* in mind. The stationery you use, the flowers you buy, even the gifts you pick out for others will reflect your new-found understanding of color.

Most important, you'll want to put *your colors* to work for you at home. Why live in less-than-flattering surroundings when you can so easily extend those colors from your closet to your walls and furnishings? By presenting yourself against the most flattering background possible, you will create a natural habitat for yourself that is as becoming as your clothes. Moreover, you will be expressing a new sense of personal style that claims the space as very much your own.

Think of the most memorable rooms you've ever visited. They probably told you a great deal about the people who lived there . . . about their likes and loves, what they value and where they've traveled, and how they spend their private hours. Paige Rense, who has built *Architectural Digest* into an arbiter of design taste, believes "A memorable personality projects a memorable style . . . of thinking, of living, of personal expression."

A successfully decorated room *is* much greater than the sum of its parts . . . it makes a personal statement about its inhabitants. Why else do we enjoy playing *voyeur* as we turn the pages of decorating magazines? We're interested in how other people live, not merely in how they fill the spaces in their homes.

There's yet another good reason for surrounding yourself with *your colors at home.* You'll *feel* more comfortable, more attractive, more relaxed and at-home, literally, in colors you're in harmony with. While others may *see* the difference, you will *sense* it.

Between now and the end of this book, we'll show you how to take the colors that make you look and feel terrific when you wear them, and use them to decorate the important areas of your home. We will make it easy for you to create backgrounds against which you will look and feel terrific *all* the time.

But what about the people with whom you share that living space? We'll tell you how to handle that, too. Plus, there's a lot of backbone decorating information between these covers. Not only will you learn how to use *your colors*, you'll learn the magic of color and the wonders it can work in your rooms. We will also explore the principles of good room arrangements and the secrets of buying wisely when it comes to choosing the furnishings that go into those arrangements.

Finally, you will become more aware of something you already know— that a beautiful home is no accident. It takes both inspiration and careful, thoughtful planning.

CHAPTER I

The Seasonal Color Theory in Brief

The concept of color types, or "seasons," has been around for a number of years. Credit for its origin has been attributed to several sources, including Johannes Itten, artist and well-known colorist at the famous Bauhaus in Germany, Suzanne Caygill, founder of the Academy of Color in San Francisco in 1942, and Gerri Pinckney and Marge Swenson, who began the Fashion Academy of Costa Mesa, California, in 1972.

Perhaps the most innovative of the color theorists is Norma Virgin of Beauty for All Seasons. In 1976, expanding on her studies in fashion and design, she founded the small color consulting company that has now grown to include more than 13,000 trained consultants.

By far the best known is Carole Jackson, whose *Color Me Beautiful* (Acropolis Books Ltd., 1980) popularized the four-season theory throughout the country with help from her nationwide network of color and image consultants.

Ms. Jackson holds that people whose skins have blue undertones are either Winters or Summers, and that those whose skins have yellow undertones (not to be confused with sallowness) are either Autumns or Springs. To be a bit more specific, Winters are generally darker overall, or have dramatic contrast between the color of their skin, eyes, and hair. Summers are fairer, with visible pink to their skin. Springs are the fairest and most delicate-looking overall. Autumns share the same general coloring as Springs, except that it's more intense.

Variations on the theme abound. Notable among them is the Color Key Program developed by the late Robert C. Dorr a half-century ago. Dorr divided all colors into two basic categories: those with a blue undertone ("Key I"), and those with a yellow undertone ("Key II"). He maintained that you are either a Key I type, with cool, blue undertones to your skin, or a Key II type, with warm, yellow undertones. Under no circumstances, he warned, should a Key I person get involved with Key II colors, and vice versa.

Leatrice Eiseman, in her *Alive With Color* (Acropolis Books Ltd., 1983), arrives at three categories in her Color Clock system, each corresponding to a different time of day: Sunrise (A.M.), Sunlight (Midday), and Sunset (P.M.). The category you fall into depends not only on your physical characteristics but also your emotional response to the colors associated with the sunrise (pure, clean, transparent, or frosty with cool, blue undertones), or with the sunset (fiery or deep, with rich, golden undertones). Midday colors are muted and subtly soft, as they look under a strong noontime sun.

Finding Your Season

Don't be put off by all the different names and theories. They all have two basic—and reliable—principles in common:

1. Your <u>skin</u> has either <u>cool (blue)</u> or warm (yellow) undertones.

2. It's those <u>undertones</u> that make you look better in certain colors than others; specifically, colors that also share that cool or warm characteristic.

How do you find out whether your category is warm or cool? It *is* possible for you to do a self-analysis, and we'll tell you more about it in a moment. However, we would strongly urge that you seek the advice of a trained color analyst/image consultant, instead. They're certainly not hard to find these days. In the Eighties, our collective preoccupation with ourselves—our health, our bodies, our looks—has created an entirely new career category:

image consulting. It's a newly opened door through which thousands of women and men are stepping into their own businesses all across the country. Finding a color and image analyst has become as easy as flipping to the classified section of your phone book (or see Resources at the end of the book). Or ask your friends. They'll probably give you the scoop on several different consultants who adhere to different systems. Which one is right for you depends on *you*, just as choosing a doctor, dentist, or hairdresser is a personal decision.

The main thing: do have a professional color consultation if you can. It will take you an hour or so, and cost from $50 to double that, depending on where you live and the analyst you choose. But, remember, this is a once-in-a-lifetime investment. The information you buy will pay for itself again and again as you shop for clothes, for makeup and hair coloring products, and for furnishings for your home. You're ahead of the game if it stops you from buying just one wrong-colored winter coat, let alone a houseful of wrong wall-to-wall carpeting.

There are two major reasons we vote for professional analysis over doing it yourself:

1. *Experience.* The trained consultant can compare your skin and its color responses with hundreds of others whom she (or he) has seen.

2. *Draping.* A professional consultant has professional tools: shawl-sized samples of fabrics color-keyed to each season. With your hair pulled back and your face free of any makeup, the consultant will drape your neck and shoulders in one color at a time to judge the overall effect. Your skin will either spark to the color, lighting up your face, or the draped color will take over and drain your natural coloring away. As you sit through the draping, you'll quickly discover which colors are great on you ... which are good ... just okay ... or downright disastrous! There's just no other way to get the same results as reliably.

However, you needn't be doomed to a colorless life if you can't find (or afford) a professional color consultant. As we promised earlier, it *is* possible to conduct a reasonably successful evaluation of yourself. You'll need three things:

1. A mirror

2. Daylight

3. The tests on the next few pages

Set the mirror up by a window so you can study your skin tones closely. No makeup allowed; you are looking for the undertones, the basic hue that lies beneath the surface of the skin. It may not be easy for you to pinpoint, especially if you're not accustomed to working with the subtleties of color. Carole Jackson of *Color Me Beautiful* suggests that if you can't get a fix on your undertones by studying your face, you should examine your wrist by holding it over a very white piece of paper. If you're still not sure, check the rest of your body, especially the parts you hide beneath a bathing suit, which never get tanned, she says. Those areas retain the skin tones that are really *you*, the ones by which you can truly judge your color category, or season.

Sometimes it helps to study the varieties of "whites" offered on most paint charts. Ivory (or antique white or candlelight white) leans toward yellow, and ice white (or bright white or cool white, etc.) has blue undertones. Visit a good paint store and bring home a color card or a range of color chips of whites. You'll easily see the difference. And, it can help you see the difference in your own skin's undertones.

Winter

Most of us are Winters. We have blue, or cool, undertones to our skins, which means we spark to colors that have the same cool, basic hues.

A Winter's skin can be anything from taupe-beige, light-to-dark rose beige, light-to-dark olive, brown or black. Or it can be white, cool white.

There's as much variety in hair and eyes, too. A Winter may have hair that's medium-to-dark brown—it can even have red highlights—or it may be coal black. A Winter's eyes can vary from brown-black to hazel, with all shades of brown in between. Gray-blue, violet-blue, gray-green, yellow-green, and turquoise eyes are also possible in Winters.

Beyond sheer numbers, what sets this season apart is its drama. Winters look terrific in sharp contrasts. Think of Elizabeth Taylor or Joan Collins. Both of them instinctively wear the kind of sharp, cool colors that set off their skin and dark hair. Could you imagine either of them looking so dramatic, so decisive, wearing colors that are muted? Winters can stand the challenge of extroverted colors. They literally vibrate to the contrast.

Because Winters do vary so much, it may be difficult for you to pick this category at first glance. When in doubt, open your closet door and study the clothes you've acquired. If two-thirds of your wardrobe is in bright, strong colors that have a blue base, then without a doubt, you're a Winter.

Some other well-known Winters: Connie Selleca, Jaclyn Smith, Cher, Audrey Hepburn, Liza Minnelli, Diahann Carroll.

Winter Color Clues

If you're a Winter, the basic color of your skin will be one of the following:

- White
- Light-to-dark taupe-beige
- Light-to-dark rose-beige
- Light-to-dark olive
- Light-to-dark taupe-brown
- Light-to-dark rose-brown
- Light-to-dark olive-brown
- Black

Your eyes are likely to be:

- Light-to-dark brown *Green*
- Brown-black
- Gray-blue
- Violet-blue
- Gray-green
- Yellow-green
- Turquoise
- Hazel (gray-brown with green or blue)

Your hair will be one of these colors (only your natural color counts):

- Black
- Brown-black
- Medium-to-dark ash brown
- Medium brown with red highlights
- Silver-gray

Summer

Summers have the same cool, blue undertones to their skins as Winters. But where a Winter's skin could be white, taupe-beige, light-to-dark rose-beige, olive, brown or black, a Summer's will be softer: light beige, light beige with pink, pink, or light-to-medium rose-beige.

Overall, Summers have softer coloring with less dramatic contrast between their skin, hair, and eyes. Therefore, they look their best in colors and color schemes that have less contrast than Winters. A Summer might be a brunette, with hair ranging from light to dark brown (always with an ashen overtone, rather than warm and golden), but the total effect is more subtle than a brunette Winter. Queen Elizabeth is a Summer with dark hair. Compare your mind's eye picture of her with a true Winter (Elizabeth Taylor), and you immediately sense the difference.

Summer's eyes are also more subtle in hue than a Winter's, although the two seasons have many colors in common. Despite our warning that eyes are only a secondary clue to your season, if you're vacillating between Winter and Summer, check them out carefully. Medium or dark brown eyes, or eyes that are brown-black definitely tip the vote to Winter. Eyes that are blue or gray-blue, green or gray-green, aqua, light gray, hazel, or light brown may peg you as a Summer.

Some other well-known Summers: Princess Di, Candice Bergen, Glenn Close, Faye Dunaway, Jane Pauley, Linda Evans.

Summer Color Clues

Although the undertones of a Summer's skin are always blue, its color will be one of the following:

- Light beige
- Light beige with pink cheeks
- Very pink
- Light-to-medium rose-beige

A Summer's eyes will probably be either:

- Blue
- Gray-blue
- Green
- Gray-green
- Light gray
- Aqua
- Hazel (blue or green with brown)
- Light brown

If your natural hair color is listed below, you are likely to be a Summer:

- Light-to-medium ash blonde
- Light-to-dark ash brown
- Medium brown with auburn highlights
- Ash-gray

Autumn

Once again, Nature calls the color shots: Autumns personify their season with coloring based on rich, yellow undertones, often crowned with glowing reds.

An Autumn's skin can be ivory, light-to-dark peach, or light-to-dark golden beige. Hair colors run the gamut of reds, from bright to copper and chestnut. An Autumn may also have medium-to-dark golden blonde or golden brown hair, or even have charcoal tresses. And when an Autumn's hair turns gray, it keeps the golden tones that characterize this season.

Don't look for blue eyes in an Autumn: you'll find turquoise or hazel, brown or green, but never a true blue or even a grayed blue.

Although there are fewer in number, you'll find some well-knowns in the Autumn category. Lucille Ball is an exhuberant example. So are Carol Burnett and Shirley MacLaine. These three have more in common than their coloring, thereby offering another clue if you're hovering between the Spring and Autumn categories. While both seasons share the basic golden undertone to their skins, you'd seldom call an Autumn *delicate*. A better word would be natural. Springs go with the clear, fresh colors of spring flowers; Autumns, with the rich, sun-warmed colors of fall—the browns, rusts, and greens with a patina of gray or gold.

Some other well-known Autumns: Diane Keaton, Lynn Redgrave, Toni Tenille, Ann-Margret, Lauren Bacall, Katharine Hepburn.

Autumn Color Clues

An Autumn's skin tones are best described as:

- Ivory
- Light-to-dark peach
- Light-to-dark golden beige
- Light-to-dark golden brown

If you're an Autumn, your eyes are likely to be:

- Light-to-dark brown
- Green
- Gold-green
- Amber
- Turquoise
- Hazel (golden brown with green)

These hair colors are pretty predictable on an Autumn:

- Red
- Copper
- Chestnut
- Medium-to-dark golden blonde
- Medium-to-dark golden brown
- Charcoal black
- Golden gray

Spring

Like Autumns, Springs are characterized by warm—or yellow—undertones to their skin. The easiest way to isolate a Spring is to think of Spring itself. It's the season that brings forth the clearest, brightest colors of the year. And when it comes to seasonal color categories, Springs follow suit, with the most delicate complexions and the brightest, clearest eye colors.

Don't let the word "delicate" fool you, however. That may apply to your own coloring, but not to the colors that best bring out your natural beauty. They are crisp and clear, as definite in their way as Winter's colors, only Spring's are warm and bright in contrast to Winter's cool, sharp palette.

All Springs have delicate ivory, peach, peach-pink, or light-to-medium peach-beige skin, whether the hair that goes with it is blonde (flaxen or strawberry), or auburn, golden brown, or gone-gray with golden overtones. Typically, a Spring's eyes are clear blue, blue-gray, green, aqua, amber, or light brown.

Marilyn Monroe was a Spring. That's why she could change Norma Jean's medium-brown hair so successfully into the smashing blonde confection that went with her stardom. Her skin tone never changed.

Some other well-known Springs: Sally Struthers, Sandra Dee, Goldie Hawn, Shirley Jones, Debbie Reynolds, Helen Hayes.

Spring Color Clues

A Spring's skin can be any of these:

- Ivory
- Peach
- Peach-pink
- Light-to-medium peach-beige

Eyes fall into the following categories:

- Blue
- Blue-gray
- Green
- Aqua
- Amber
- Light brown

If you are a Spring, your hair is likely to be a natural:

- Light-to-medium flaxen blonde
- Strawberry blonde
- Auburn
- Light-to-medium golden brown
- Pearl gray

Your Colors At Home

Distinctive rooms have always expressed distinct color personalities. That's because the people who inhabit them have distinct personalities themselves. For example, think of Diana Vreeland, long the driving *energy* behind *Vogue* and now the creator of must-see costume shows at the Metropolitan Museum of Art. Could you for a moment imagine her living in quiet, all-beige surroundings? Even if you've met the amazing Miss Vreeland only on the printed page, you must think of her in color. And that color is *red*, of course, an almost startling, bright red that plays dramatic counterpoint to the black hair and white skin that mark her as a Winter.

"Red is the great clarifier—bright, cleansing, and revealing," Miss Vreeland writes. "I can't imagine becoming bored with red—it would be like becoming bored with the person you love."

When the color is right, right for you, you don't become bored with it. You come to be associated with it. That color becomes your signature. Take JoAnn Barwick, editor of *House Beautiful*, for another example. She's a Summer who is renowned for her affinity for soft blues, and the entire home fashions industry understands that if you want a room published in *House Beautiful*, it better have lots of blue. Yet, in spite of the fact that she sits in such a taste-making position as the editor of a long-important magazine, JoAnn is quick to encourage others to find their individual styles and follow them.

"The '80s is the decade of the individual, and her choice reigns supreme," she says. "We're in an era where rules can be broken, where no one look dominates, and all options are open. If we have the courage of our convictions, then style can be ours."

This book will help you express the courage of your color convictions and find your personal style in the decor of your home. You will need to be brave, make no mistake about that. Decorating has always caused a faint tremble in the bottom of even the most stalwart hearts. Decisions about style and color that we can make for *ourselves* in a split-second, without a backward glance, become monumental when they're going to be spread out over an entire room for the proverbial world to see. It's not unheard of for one professional interior designer to consult another, to *hire* another, even, to do their

personal living spaces. Hairdressers do each other's hair all the time ...
doctors avoid treating family members, so it's not all that unusual for an
interior designer to reach out for a second opinion.

The point, of course, is that it takes a combination of courage and
expertise to design and furnish a room, for at least three very good reasons.
One, you'll be spending a fair amount of money; *two,* you'll be living with your
decisions for a long time to come; *three,* your personal taste will indeed be on
the line for the world to see. And comment upon. A word about that now
(more later on when we discuss how to cope with other color personalities
under your roof). You are *not* creating this room for the world to live in; you
are creating it for you and whomever you love enough to share it with. If the
room works for you and for them, if you enjoy being there, living with the
colors and things you have chosen, then that room is a success. Never mind
the opinions of others; you'll do better to listen to the advice of E. B. White,
the oft-quoted author of *The Elements of Style.* While he may have been
concerned with style in writing, his wisdom also rings true for home
decorators embarking on a project: "... approach style warily, realizing that it
is yourself you are approaching, no other ...."

Keep White's advice very much in mind as you choose among *your colors*
for your decorating theme. In many cases, remember, these are not orthodox
decorating colors, not what you're used to seeing outside your wardrobe.
That's what makes the idea of using *your colors,* the colors that make you look
and feel terrific, so fresh, new, and highly individual. A while back, there was
an invigorating series on public television called "The Shock of the New." The
word "shock" may be a bit strong in this context, but the new *is* often
surprising. Be assured that you are in for some surprises, and that all of them
can be positive if you approach your decorating project with the courage of
your conviction that *your colors* are the right colors to live with, as well as to
wear.

For this age of the individual, we are updating the rules on color. Color
facts don't change, of course, just as the basic facts of life never change. But
what behavior-expert Letitia Baldridge has done for etiquette in her contemporary revision of Emily Post's classic, bringing manners up to date, we've set
out to do for the use of color.

All this is meant to reassure you. Decorating has often been a peculiarly unnerving venture to many people, which is illogical when you realize that shelter—home—is a basic need for all of us. We all need chairs to sit on, beds to sleep in, lights to read by, tables to put things on when we sit down to eat or work. Fly over any city on a clear day, and you'll look down on thousands of roof-tops, under each of which is an assortment of furnishings. Some are put together so that they look and function well, others aren't. The difference, it seems logical to suppose, lies in the self-confidence of the people who put all these objects together. If you've lacked that self-confidence up to now, you might blame old Louis XIV of France.

We have a pet theory that the Sun King threw a very long shadow over the entire subject of interior decorating when he set out to make Versailles Palace the showplace of the world. Louis brought in the finest craftsmen and artists from all over Europe, and orchestrated their work into astonishingly ornate interiors. To this day, half the terms in the language of interior design are French—words such as *fauteuil* (armchair), *chaise longue* (long chair), and even *foyer* (entrance hall). In less sophisticated times, the terminology of interior design may have been a bit intimidating for anyone whose textbook French had gone rusty.

Happily, today that's all changing. We've democratized the terms and simplified the processes to put beautiful rooms within everyone's reach. And now, you can even narrow your color options down to *your colors*. Since you already know what great results to expect when wearing *your colors*, you're virtually assured of success when your decorating project is finished. Besides, you'll have fun along the way. Nothing gives you a fresher perspective on life than a newly decorated room. If that's the "shock" of the new, then it's really quite delightful.

Understanding Your Colors

As you will see on the next few pages, within your season you must choose the colors that best suit you personally. Each palette has light colors and bright colors. Remember that the coloring of individuals within each season varies in intensity. Most of us look good in all of our colors, but depending on the depth of our skin and hair color, some colors look better than others. For example, if you are very fair, you may find that some of your colors are too bright. If you have stronger coloring, your very light colors or neutrals may be too weak.

Finding Your Best Colors

Winters are best in the true and primary colors, as well as their darker, bluer shades. Think *true, blue, and vivid*. The very fair Winter is most flattered by the icy or deep colors; the Winter with darker skin is better in brighter colors. Winters should avoid any color with a yellow undertone. Brown is another no-no unless it's dark enough to look almost black. Winter is the only season that looks good in pure white or black.

Summers are best in pastels and soft neutrals. Think *blue, pink, and soft*. The very fair blonde Summer is complemented by light colors; brunette Summers are better in the deeper shades of their palette. Summers should avoid pure white, black, or any color with a yellow undertone.

Autumns are best in the rich colors of fall. Think *earthy, yellow, and intense*. The very fair Autumn is better in the more muted shades; the Autumn with darker skin looks better in bright colors, too drab in earth tones. Autumns should avoid pure white, black, navy, gray, pink, and any color with a blue undertone.

Springs are best in crisp colors. Think *clear, yellow, and bright*. The very fair Spring can be overwhelmed by bright colors; the Spring with more definite coloring is better in bright colors, too pale in light colors. Springs should avoid pure white, black, and any color with a blue undertone.

The Eyes Have It

With all the wonderful, workable colors and color combinations in your palette, how do you go about narrowing down your choices?

One answer is easier than you might have thought. Go with the colors that play up your eyes.

You can emphasize your eyes by using more of their *same* color, and then bringing on *contrasting* colors. Blue eyes are complemented by yellows or oranges. Green eyes are complemented by reds or red-oranges. Never mind that there is no true complement for gray, or dark brown eyes—both bright colors and white will set them off beautifully.

CHAPTER II

Create a New World Filled with Your Colors

Beauty *is* skin-deep when it comes to creating the perfect setting for *you*. The clue to your most flattering color schemes and decorating styles can be found right in your own skin tone. Although each one of us is unique, we all belong to one of four "seasons." It's easy to see the difference between the seasons: Winters and Summers have cool, blue undertones to their skins; Autumns and Springs have warm, yellow undertones. In decorating your home, choose colors that share your own blue or yellow undertones, and play up your natural beauty.

What Season Are You?

How do you find out if you are a Winter, Summer, Autumn, or Spring? It *is* possible for you to do a self-analysis, but we urge you to seek the advice of a trained color consultant. The information you buy will pay for itself again and again as you shop for clothes, for makeup and hair coloring products, and for furnishings for your home.

Photograph courtesy BEAUTY FOR ALL SEASONS

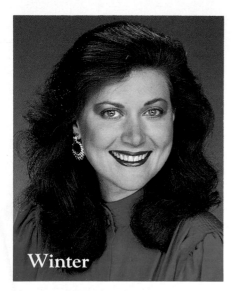

Winter

A typical Winter looks best in rooms decorated in the medium-to-dark colors of her palette. The icy colors should be mixed in prints or used in accents.

The Icy, Vivid Colors of Winter

If there is one word to describe a Winter, it is *dramatic.* That applies to personality and style, as well as looks. Winters are dynamic, love adventure, and are fond of the grand gesture. Underneath all this, however, Winters are usually cooly logical, with a strong sense of self and of purpose. In short, Winters are as definite about life as their colors are sharp. Even the neutrals that work best for Winters have a sharp quality about them...the light colors in her palette are icy...and there's no mistaking Winter's white: it's as clear and blue-white as snow.

Winters look wonderful in rooms filled with color, or conversely, in all white rooms accented here and there with a few dynamite colors. Winters opt for high drama in decorating, with sharp contrasts, such as black-and-white marble floors and such grand gestures as sweeping staircases, mahogany four-poster beds, or an ultra-contemporary ambience sparked with chrome, glass, and lacquered walls.

Wood Colors and Finishes

In a word, a Winter's best woods are dark with fine graining and a highly polished finish.

Painted woods should be white, or the true colors of Winter's palette.

Winter's best metal is silver, or silver-toned.

White

Icy Gray

Light True Gray

Medium True Gray

Charcoal Gray

Icy Taupe

Taupe

Royal Blue

Navy   MIDNIGHT - ALMOST BLACK

Black

True Red

Icy Pink

Icy Yellow

Icy Green

Icy Emerald

Icy Turquoise

Icy Aqua

Icy Blue

Icy Periwinkle

Icy Violet

Blue Red

Strawberry Pink

Light True Yellow

Light True Green

Light Emerald Green

Light Turquoise

Light Aqua Blue

Light True Blue

Light Periwinkle

Light True Purple

Bright Burgundy

Fuchsia

True Yellow

True Green

Emerald Green

Turquoise

Aqua Blue

True Blue

Periwinkle

Royal Purple

35

A typical Summer's best rooms are decorated in the light-to-medium colors of her palette. The darker colors should be used as accents, or mixed in prints.

The Powdery, Cool Colors of Summer

Just as Nature originally planned it, Summers are a softer version of Winter. The same cool, blue tones underlie Summer's palette, and contrast is again a key word in planning color schemes. Only with Summers, the contrast is lighter, less resounding, more refined. That's because Summers are classics: calm, composed, and very much in control. No grand gestures needed, no clarion colors or dramatic statements. Summer's best colors are muted, gentled versions of Winter's attention-demanding palette. Pretend you are out in a summer flower garden with its kaleidoscope of colors, only it's cool and misty—everything is slightly hushed. That goes for Summer's white, too. It's cool and softly "off-white."

Summer's natural habitat is often based on large doses of that white. Contrasting schemes work well for Summers, too, as long as the colors don't jolt each other visually. There's nothing ever loud or demanding about a Summer; her rooms are comfortable and relaxing, likely to be filled with period pieces—possibly French—and decidedly feminine.

Wood Colors and Finishes

Woods with ashen overtones and low-gloss finishes are best for a Summer's rooms.

Painted woods should be off-white, a neutral, or one of your light colors.

Summer's best metal is silver or rose-gold.

Off-White

Light Rose Beige

Medium Rose Beige

Rose Beige

Rose Brown

Light Blue Gray

Medium Blue Gray

Blue Gray

Gray Blue

Grayed Navy

Powder Pink

Petal Pink

Soft Yellow

Mint Green

Soft Aqua

Powder Blue

Soft Periwinkle

Lilac

Soft Mauve

Soft Orchid

Pink-Pink

Rose Pink

Yellow

Emerald Green

Aqua Blue

Sky Blue

Periwinkle

Lavender

Mauve

Orchid

Dusty Pink

Dusty Rose

Dusty Yellow

Dusty Emerald

Dusty Aqua

Dusty Blue

Dusty Periwinkle

Dusty Lavender

Dusty Mauve

Dusty Orchid

Autumn

A typical Autumn is best in rooms decorated in the medium-to-dark colors of her palette. The lighter colors should be used as accents, or mixed in prints.

The Warm, Earthy Colors of Autumn

All the clues to an Autumn's best colors are summed up in the season itself. Think of mellow days when the warm sunshine slants through blazing leaves overhead... think of "September Morn" with the mists rising softly from the water... and think of football mums, hunting scenes, and long walks in the country, wearing tweeds with leather elbow patches.

Autumns, with their natural golden glow and affinity for the outdoors, are the personification of everything that makes this season so appealing. Indoors, that attitude translates into rooms you feel instantly at home in: friendly, welcoming, and very easy to relax in.

Autumn's are earth colors in the richest possible sense—those deep, warm hues that often turn up in Constable paintings. In fact, you wouldn't be far off to think of an Autumn in Old English terms. She's likely to favor oak and pine furniture and to love such personality pieces as a hunt table or a huge Welsh cupboard.

Wood Colors and Finishes

The best woods for an Autumn are medium-to-dark brown with a low-gloss or antiqued finish.

Painted woods should be oyster, neutrals, or medium-to-dark colors.

Autumn's best metal is antiqued brass.

Oyster White

Light Warm Beige

Medium Warm Beige

Warm Beige

Camel

Medium Camel

Rust

Coffee

Milk Chocolate

Dark Chocolate

Bisque

Peach

Apricot

Light Gold

Light Avocado

Light Moss

Light Jade

Light Turquoise

Aqua Blue

Light Periwinkle

Light Red-Orange

Light Tangerine

Light Orange

Medium Gold

Medium Avocado Green

Medium Moss Green

Medium Jade Green

Medium Turquoise

Light Teal Blue

Medium Periwinkle

Red-Orange

Tangerine

Orange

Gold

Avocado Green

Moss Green

Jade Green

Turquoise

Teal Blue

Periwinkle

Spring

A typical Spring looks best in rooms decorated in the light-to-medium colors of her palette. The darker colors should be used mixed in prints, or used as accents.

The Warm, Bright Colors of Spring

Spring practically leaps to the eye. Its color message is fresh, bright, clear and everywhere laced with the cheery yellow of April sunshine.

It follows that many Springs are vivacious, determined to be where the action is. That includes home, since rooms done in Spring's crisp colors are inherently alive and sunny. Even Spring's white is invigorated with sunshine.

Look for a touch of whimsy in her interiors, too, such as an amusing Victorian piece. A Spring tends to be romantic, the kind of very feminine woman who sleeps in a canopy bed, lavishes ruffles on her boudoir chaise, and wallcovers her entire bath in bright flowers.

Even when her tastes are more tailored, you'd never find a Spring at home with sleek, hard-edged contemporary. Springs are more interested in fun than formality. They may be sophisticated enough to pair painted chairs with a scrubbed pine dining table, but it will be done with unselfconscious ease. Any room a Spring calls home is insouciant and charming.

Wood Colors and Finishes

The best wood colors for a Spring are light golden blonde to medium golden brown, with a semi-gloss finish.

Painted woods should be ivory, or in Spring's bright colors.

Spring's best metal is polished brass.

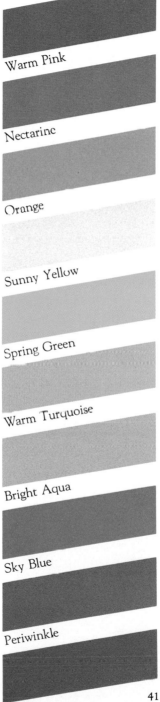

Ivory

Light Warm Beige

Medium Warm Beige

Warm Beige

Light Camel

Milk Chocolate

Light Dove Gray

Medium Dove Gray

Dove Gray

Clear Navy

Shell Pink

Peach

Apricot

Light Yellow

Light Green

Light Turquoise

Light Aqua

Light Blue

Light Periwinkle

Lavender

Light Warm Pink

Light Nectarine

Light Orange

Light Sunny Yellow

Light Spring Green

Light Warm Turquoise

Light Bright Aqua

Light Sky Blue

Medium Periwinkle

Light Violet

Warm Pink

Nectarine

Orange

Sunny Yellow

Spring Green

Warm Turquoise

Bright Aqua

Sky Blue

Periwinkle

Violet

41

As complicated as it may look at first glance, the color wheel is really nothing more than an ingenious way to help us understand the magic we're working with.

By studying the wheel, you can see for yourself where all the colors in the world come from, and how they react to each other. The wheel will make it easier for you to plan a color scheme around *your* colors since you can see the difference between the *warm* colors, with their yellow undertone, and those that are *cool*, with a blue undertone. It's this vital difference that makes the entire Seasonal Color Theory work so beautifully.

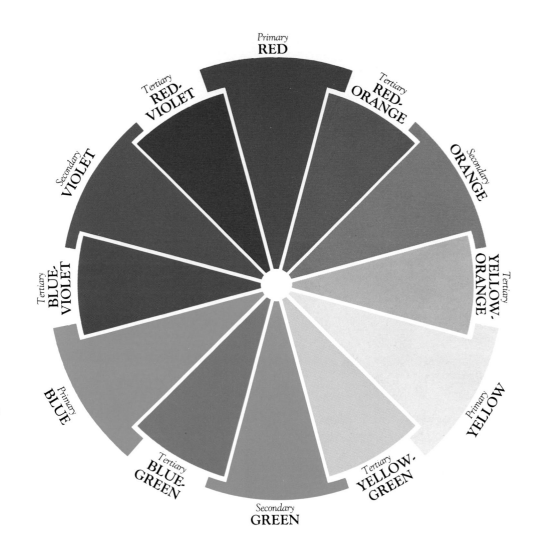

Primary Colors

Red, yellow, and blue are the primary colors. These colors are pure. They cannot be created by mixing other colors; rather, they are the sources of all the other colors we see.

Secondary Colors

Orange, green, and violet are the secondary colors. They are created by mixing equal parts of each of the two primary colors on either side of them on the color wheel. Each secondary color is the complement of the primary that lies directly across from it on the color wheel.

Tertiary Colors

Tertiary colors are created by mixing equal parts of a primary and the secondary color that lies next to it. Now, we are beginning to get into the subtle gradations—red-orange, yellow-orange, yellow-green, blue-green, blue-violet, red-violet—that eventually produce all the 10 million or so different colors the human eye can distinguish.

MAGENTA

BLACK

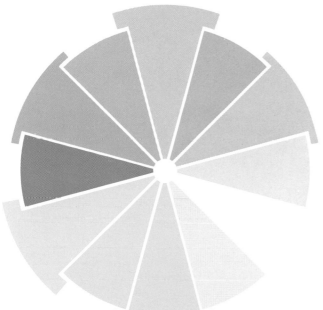

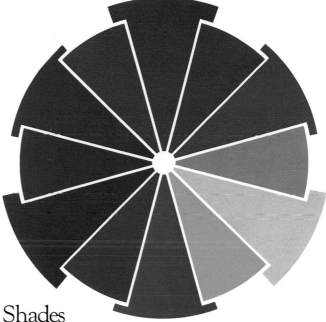

Tints

Another dimension of the color wheel involves tints and shades, that is, the *lightness* or *darkness* of a color. Here, the colors have all been lightened by adding 50 percent white, so they are pastels or tints. The lighter the tint, the more compatible it becomes, so that even contrasting colors can be made to work quietly with each other.

Shades

Going in the opposite direction and adding 50 percent black to the colors on the wheel creates shades, or the darkened version of the basic colors. It's this ability to vary colors up and down the scale of lightness and saturation that produces the almost infinite variety you have to work with in decorating your home.

Contrasting Colors

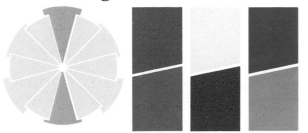

Because the seasonal system offers a new way of working with colors, your complementary decorating schemes may not always be built around actual complements, that is, the colors that lie directly opposite each other on the color wheel. They may not represent the best color choices for your season; therefore, you'll want to find the actual complement and then adjust the color, according to your own palette. *(See Page 62.)*

Related Colors

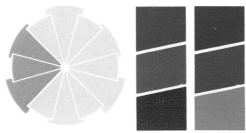

Left:
Blue, blue-violet, and violet is an example of an analogous color scheme.

Right:
Blue, medium blue, and light blue is an example of a monochromatic color scheme.

Related colors can be either monochromatic—various shades of the same color—or analogous—those near to each other on the wheel. Related colors that are monochromatic are easier to use when decorating a room that must suit people of different seasons.

The Season Spanners

What if you share home space—but not seasons—with the other people in your life?

There are three colors that can be flattering to everyone. They are:

- Aqua
- Periwinkle
- Coral Pink

Almost everyone looks good in schemes based on one of these colors when they're liberally laced with white. Whose white? Probably the all-around best compromise between seasons is the off-white of Summer.

There are several ways to use the Season-Spanners. You might pick everyone's favorite and use it with off-white . . . or, try a related scheme of aqua and periwinkle with off-white, or a contrasting scheme of coral pink and either aqua or periwinkle and off-white . . . or find a print that has all three colors on an off-white background.

For more variety in planning season-spanning schemes, study the other palettes and look for colors you may have in common with other seasons under your roof.

Aqua   *Periwinkle*   *Coral Pink*

CHAPTER III

Color—
Your Most Vital Ally
in Decorating

Working with Colors

The human eye, we're told, can pick out approximately 10 million variations in color. That would amount to a veritable *bewilderment* of riches for the home decorator if it were not for Sir Isaac Newton, who created the color wheel. Working around the color wheel, and back and forth across it, we can easily see how those variations in color evolve, and understand how all those different colors affect each other.

Forget for a moment that you are concerned mainly with *your colors*, the ones that will show you off to best advantage at home. It is important for you to develop at least a working knowledge of how colors behave in general— physically, optically, and emotionally—when they are mixed in varying proportions and seen under various conditions. It will also be helpful for you to become conversant with the vocabulary of color, so that eventually you and your paint dealer, interior designer, or carpet salesperson will all be speaking the same language.

Here, then, is a *color primer*, an introduction to (or refresher course in) colors and how they work. Coming up a few pages later, we'll tell you how to apply all this to *your colors* when you are building a color scheme for your home.

Around the Color Wheel

All 10 million or so of the colors we are able to perceive begin with just three: red, yellow, and blue. Since every other color under the sun can be made by combining this trio in varying amounts, they are logically known as the *primary colors*. Sir Isaac started laying out his color wheel by spacing these three equidistantly around the perimeter. The spaces between he filled with the colors that result when you mix equal parts of two primary colors: red plus yellow equals orange . . . yellow plus blue equals green . . . blue plus red equals violet. Orange, green, and violet, therefore, are known as the *secondary colors*. When you take equal parts of these secondary colors and mix them with the primary color that lies nearest to each on the color wheel, you come up with the *tertiary colors*.

The tertiaries are the third generation colors: red-orange, yellow-orange, yellow-green, blue-green, blue-violet, and red-violet. Tertiary is a phrase you may come across in your adventures with color, but you'll probably never need it. Likewise, from the tertiary colors you could go on mixing until you reach the fourth generation, or *quaternary* levels, and eventually arrive at all 10 million variations we're capable of seeing. However, our purpose here is to simplify the principles of using a few special colors—*your colors*—successfully in your home.

There are several other words that belong in your decorating vocabulary:

- *Hue* is simply another word for color. For example, the hue of your ginger jar lamp could be emerald green.

- *Intensity* refers to how much color is in a color; that is, how green is that emerald green. It could be a pale emerald, or a deep, intense emerald. Both are officially green; the difference is in their intensity.

- *Value* has to do with the inherent lightness or darkness of a color relative to all other colors. For example, yellow has a higher value than green, green has a higher value than purple, etc.

- *Tint* refers to how much white a color has in it. The handy umbrella word that covers all tints is *pastel*. Pastels are close to white and rank very high on the value scale.

- *Shades*, on the other hand, are those colors down the value scale, closer to black. Lilac is a pastel; royal purple goes to the other extreme, deeply shaded with black.

- *Texture*, or *finish*, is another important dimension of color that has decided effects on how dark or light it appears. A lustrous, shiny finish will make a color look lighter than the same color with a dull or matte finish. That's why the silk pillow you buy to match a velvet sofa will look brighter and lighter when you toss it on. It's just one of the many little optical illusions you will come to expect of color, and learn to deal with in advance.

Four Basic Ways to Set A Color Scheme

There are a number of time-tested and proven ways to go about establishing an attractive color scheme for a room. Some of them can get rather esoteric, involving fancy footwork around the color wheel and talk of "split-complementaries," "triadic" combinations, and the like.

We believe that the simplest way is the surest way to build a successful color scheme. Since you already know which colors you will be working with—*your colors*—you've eliminated most of the upfront decision-making. Now it remains for you to decide how you're going to combine *your colors* so your rooms make you look and feel as terrific as your clothes do.

Of all the various approaches you'll find in other decorating guides, we recommend four "formulas," all easy to understand and easy to put together yourself. Just because you follow one of these standard approaches, you need not be concerned that you'll end up with an ordinary room. You'll be working with *your colors*, combining them in *your* special way, expressing *your* personal tastes and sense of style, so the room can't help but turn out to be very personally *yours*.

There are four basic ways to go about setting a color scheme for a room. Any one of them will work, no matter what your season is, as long as you interpret it in colors chosen from your palette.

The four systems we're recommending are built around colors that are either:

- Contrasting
- Related
- Neutral
- All-white, plus ...

Here's what those terms mean, and how they work in interior design:

Contrasting color schemes

As the name implies, decorative schemes based on contrasting—or complementary—colors can set a room in motion, visually speaking. Looking back at Sir Isaac's handy color wheel, we see that such complements lie in direct opposition to each other, as far away as possible across the wheel.

This means that contrasting color schemes are built on colors that are as *unalike* as they can be. Reds and greens, yellows and violets, oranges and blues are all complements, or contrasting colors. That's why when they're used together, red and green make Christmas such a visually stimulating season, yellow and violet vibrate in spring bouquets and, in autumn, an orange leaf stands out against a blue sky. Indoors, in room settings, contrasting color schemes must be used with some finesse.

Related color schemes

Related color schemes can be either "monochromatic"—variations of the same color—or "analogous"—those near each other on the wheel. Either way, the colors are related and, as in any good family situation, the relations get on harmoniously.

Decorative schemes based on related colors are, therefore, easy to put together in the first place. Since there are no sharp shifts between color notes to jar the eye and senses, even the inexperienced home decorator can't go far wrong putting related colors together because they inherently have so much in common. In most cases, related schemes based on monochromatic colors are easiest to build from the seasonal palettes. And they're definitely the best choice when you're decorating to suit people of different seasons.

Neutral color schemes

This is the fail-safe way to orchestrate the "un-colors"—browns, beiges, taupes, grays, and whites—into a scheme that's naturally calm and sophisticated. The word "monochromatic" may come to mind here, too. While the word itself literally means "one color," we've also come to associate it in decorating terms with the entire palette of neutral colors, played up and down the value scale and enlivened with an eye-pleasing variety of textures. Since every season's palette has its share of neutrals, this formula can be a winning scheme for every one of us.

All white, plus . . . schemes

The *plus* in this type of room-scheming is your choice of another color. Not only is this one of the simplest color formulas to follow, it's also practically failproof. The only caveat about an all-white plus decorating scheme is that it can be very dramatic. That's perfect for a Winter, who sparks to sharp color contrasts, but potentially too clarion for other seasons unless you soften the white and choose your accent colors carefully.

The Many Dimensions of Color:
Use it to Rearrange Room Space and Solve Decorating Problems

Color is a powerful force. It can push space around, stretch or shrink entire rooms, make bad features disappear, and even affect the weather *indoors*.

You can capture this marvelous power of color, and use it to great decorative advantage. But, before you get down to applying *your colors at home*, you must understand the magic you're working with and what it can do for you.

Rearrange your room space

Colors' amazing ability to push space around lets you effectively "remodel" a room at the stroke of a paint brush. Raise the roof, lower the ceiling, square off long, narrow spaces—you can do it all with colors that are cool and "receding" or warm and "advancing." Receding colors are usually content to stay in the background; the eye simply doesn't dwell on them. Light-colored surfaces, therefore, have a tendency to appear to be further away. In effect, they create the illusion of distance and space. Conversely, advancing colors move forward. They fill the eye and make spaces look fuller, more crowded. Dark colors also fall into this category.

Both optical illusions can be extremely useful. For example:

- To raise the ceiling and make a room feel more spacious, paint it a color that's light in value. If you choose a wallcovering, make it one with a light background and small, allover pattern. Or, one that has a built-in optical illusion of its own, such as an open-work trellis against a light background.

- To stretch room space itself, apply the same idea to the walls, and avoid sharp, eye-stopping contrast between the walls and woodwork or other architectural features, such as mantels and doors. Light, on-flowing colors and small, all-over patterns fool the eye into seeing more space than really exists. If you stop the eye with a sharp contrast, it subconsciously sets limits on the space. Keep this principle in mind when you're working at floor-level, too. It's the reason wall-to-wall carpeting is a good idea for small rooms, or small areas that flow into each other. An unbroken sweep of color underfoot will make the space look more generous, but this also brings us smack up against one of those funny little caprices of color we mentioned earlier. When the carpet is light in color, it tends to pop into our awareness instead of receding, as light colors do elsewhere. Light floors, whether they're carpeted, stained, or painted, will fill our field of vision and alter the proportions of the room accordingly.

- To play up architectural features, define them with color. Stain beams dark against a light ceiling, paint mouldings white against dark-toned walls, deliberately emphasize wainscoting or chair rails to make them "pop" and add visual interest to the room.

- To cozy-up a room, bring dark colors into action. Paint ceilings dark, or wallcover them with an extroverted print to bring them down in the mind's eye and make their presence felt in the room. Dark-stained beams overhead will have the same effect. Similar *legerdemain* works on walls: dark colors and strong patterns bring them forward to make the space feel closer and cozier.

- To change the dimension of a room, employ both of these visual principles. If, for instance, you have a long and awkwardly narrow room, here's how to "square" it off: color the short walls dark to bring them forward, and treat the long walls lightly so they're less imposing.

Make decorating problems disappear

Plagued with an awkward column? With a sofa that's oversized and over-bearing? Out of sight, out of mind. Color them copacetic by blending them right into their backgrounds. Paint the column and upholster the sofa to match the wall behind, and your problems will quickly disappear. Ditto for architectural irregularities in a room. Odd-ball nooks, crannies, and alcoves will flatten obligingly when you roll over them with unbroken color.

Control the mood of your room

Color, it's worth repeating, has a direct emotional effect on us. Let's consider its ability to raise or lower the overall temperature in a room, both visually and emotionally. As we've already seen, colors belong to either the warm or the cool side of the spectrum. It's not hard to guess which, as nature provides the clues. Warm colors come from sunshine: *reds, yellows, oranges.* Ice is the origin of the cools: *blues, greens, and violets.* It follows naturally that rooms with warm colors radiate an entirely different mood than those based on the cool side of the color wheel. They're likely to be more casual, more visually active and warm. All of which make them perfect for an Autumn or Spring ambience.

The cool colors, on the other hand, impart an air of sophistication, somewhat more formality, and a bit of reserve. Because these colors all have blue undertones, rooms based on the cool spectrum make automatically "right" backgrounds for Winters and Summers.

However, don't think for a moment that you'll be limited to one side of the spectrum or the other; there are cooled-down reds that work beautifully for Winters and Summers, and warm greens that make sensational settings for Autumns and Springs.

A further word about color temperatures: Once upon earlier times, we were cautioned to set color schemes according to the orientation of the room—that is, whether it faced to the cool north light, or into a warm southern exposure. The idea used to be that you should compensate for the light's excesses with the colors you used. However, the changes that have come over so many lifestyles in the late 20th century have made real daylight less important than the artificial lights you use in a room. Most of us simply aren't home that much during the day anymore.

The light fantastic

With the emphasis now shifted to the nighttime hours, what matters is the way different colors respond to those artificial lighting conditions. If yours is a working family, which means your rooms will be used primarily under the kind of lights you plug in, as opposed to daylight, then you should shop for the rooms' furnishings under the same kind of lighting conditions. Since most stores seem to favor fluorescent lighting regardless of the havoc it plays with color, *buy nothing* until you've taken home a color sample to study *in situ* under your particular lighting conditions. The rationale here is simple: since color is composed of nothing more than the way we perceive light, the source of that light becomes the catalyst. Incandescent light, by far the most popular kind found on the homefront, has a yellowish warmth not unlike natural sunlight. Fluorescents, on the other hand, are generally cold and bluish-white. Both can play astonishing games with colors. So can the kind of shades on the lamps you have in the room. If they're translucent, allowing light to pass through, you can anticipate relatively even illumination of the room and the colors therein. Opaque shades, on the other hand, focus light up and down on the ceiling or wall nearest the lamp, and on the tabletop directly beneath it. You must consider the color of the shade, the walls, ceiling and floor, and make allowances for whatever "spin" they impart to the light that's going to be bounced over the other colors in the room.

The best way to deal with these potential variables in color is to take home a large swatch to study. If it's fabric, you'd be well advised to buy a half-yard, if necessary. A few dollars spent up-front might obviate an expensive mistake later. If it's paint, buy a pint and brush on a *wide* swatch for appraisal. If it's a wallcovering, try to take home the sample book at least overnight. By living with realistic samples of the colors you are considering, you'll be able to see how they behave under different lighting conditions.

Playing with patterns
Believe us, patterns can be capricious. And in being so they can cause unpredictable problems. To wit: a small print that looks red and white at close range can come off pink at a distance, throwing your entire decorating scheme into disarray. So can a tweed rug. Up close, you may be able to discern the distinct colors that exactly match the print on your sofa. But step back to the normal viewing distance, and those "perfect" colors may look entirely different. The moral once again: invest in a sample and look at it under your individual living conditions before you decide.

Throwing colors' weight around
A final, general consideration of color—and the funny tricks it can play to lead the best-laid decorating plans astray—comes when you start plotting the arrangement of furniture within the room. Keep in mind the relative weights of colors and of patterns: dark colors and closely knit patterns "weigh" more than light colors and open-work patterns. A three-seater sofa, for example, is visually heavier when it's covered in a dark solid, or dark-grounded print, than it is wearing a light solid or light-grounded pattern. Try to balance pieces of similar weight around the room. For instance, a vertical mahogany secretary or a tall window wearing the matching print "equals" the visual weight of a sofa or grouping that includes a loveseat, table, and two chairs.

Color distribution

When you're weighing out colors and patterns in a room, it will help to have three rule-of-thumb formulas to guide you:

1. Never cluster a color or pattern on one side of the room. Use it in a major way here ... repeat it in a smaller amount over there ... with another *touch* of it there for emphasis.

2. All colors are *not* created equal and shouldn't be treated so. Choose your best color and give it the starring role, then let the other colors in your scheme play counterpoint around the room.

3. Never use a color just once, even if it's just the accent color. Always repeat it in small touches here and there—the fringe on a throw pillow, the mat on a picture, the welting on a chair—just to show you really mean it.

Apportioning colors in a room

Professional designers often subdivide a room into three areas for color-planning purposes:

1. *The dominant areas:* floors and walls
2. *The secondary areas:* windows and upholstered pieces
3. *The accent areas:* occasional chairs, lamps, and accessories

The dominant areas establish your color scheme. The colors and patterns you use here will determine the color personality of the room and its overall ambience, as well. Remember that what you apply to such large areas will assume exaggerated proportions—colors will look brighter and prints more assertive. Generally, it's a good idea to keep these areas softer and let them be the background against which you'll play the brighter colors in your scheme. A good way to handle a really exciting color is to use it to make one definite statement, on the walls or as a border in an area rug, for example. Then repeat it in the print you might use on the secondary areas, and as accent touches.

Form follows fabric

One of the easiest—and most foolproof—ways to work out the balance of colors in your room is to choose a fabric first. After all, professional artists have already established the colors for you when they designed the fabric. Choose a pattern that's based on *your colors*, then follow these steps:

- Let the fabric's background color dictate the dominant areas.

- Use the fabric itself for the secondary areas.

- Lift the fabric's most eye-catching color for accents.

Consider ready-made coordinates

Let's thank today's designers of home fashions. They've taken a lot of the worry out of putting a room together by creating entire collections—wallcovering, fabric, and even such accessories as lamps and rugs. As you shop the pages of your wallcovering sample books, you'll find coordinated prints color-harmonized so you can mix and match them with complete confidence.

**Pull A Color Scheme
From A Fabric**

The proportion of color in a print can help you establish a color scheme.

Use the background color for the room's dominant areas.

Use the fabric itself on areas of secondary importance.

Use the accent color in the fabric as the accent color for the room.

Pattern Mix—two patterns

Patterns that are very different can co-exist beautifully as long as they have a color in common.

In a bedroom, this blended floral could be used for a coverlet and the print coordinate for a bed skirt and slipper chair.

Working out your own pattern mix

Mixing patterns on your own is no mystery once you discover the magic formula for success. You can choose patterns that are as different as they can be, say, a large floral and a plaid or stripe, and make them co-exist beautifully as long as they have a common color denominator. By the same token, two patterns that are similar in design can work well together, provided they are very alike in color and very unalike in scale. A large window-pane check and a small stripe come to mind here.

Before you settle on a pattern mix, pin samples together on the wall or back of your sofa to make sure you can easily see the relationship between the two. Once you have established that essential color kinship, it's possible to introduce yet a third pattern into your scheme. For instance, a mix like this would work handsomely in a bedroom:

Pattern	Used for
Print fabric	Bed & Windows
Coordinating print fabric	Canopy & Bed Skirt
Matching wallpaper	All walls
Patterned carpet	Rug with border

There's an unexpected pleasure in discovering such close-but-not exact repetitions of a motif in a room. While the eye does crave some similarities and balance, it also grows quickly bored looking at the exact same thing. The imaginary room just described is much more vital and interesting in its variety than it would have been if only one print had been played against a background of solid colors.

The exciting exception

Deliberately *overdo* one print, using it exclusively and extensively all over a room—walls, windows, upholstered pieces or bed, everywhere—to create a cozily enveloping environment. When you're using so much of it, a small print on a light background is probably your best bet. You can upholster the walls with the same fabric you use for windows and covers, or use the matching wallcovering. A solid carpet, or a stroke or two of the major color in the print, used as accent, will provide contrast enough to satisfy the eye and prove that sometimes it's just not possible to have *too much* of a good thing.

Patterns that are similar in design can work well together as long as they are very alike in color and very unalike in scale.

In a sitting room, this blended window-pane check could be used for a love seat and coordinating stripe could be used for two chairs.

Building a Room Around Your Colors

Now that you know the range of colors—*your colors*—that you will be working with, you are almost ready to turn them into a successful decorating scheme. Before we actually get down to choosing and using specific colors for specific rooms, there are still several general criteria you must factor into the equation:

- What function will the room perform?
- Who will actually use it? When? How?
- What mood do you want to create in the room? That is, what personality do you want to establish there?
- Where do you live: in a house? In an apartment? In the city? In the suburbs? In the country?
- Where is the room itself located within your home? What kind of light, view, and traffic flow does it have?
- What is its architectural style? A definite traditional period? Clearly contemporary? Nothing special?

What will the room do, and for whom?

Before you can give a meaningful answer, you must evaluate and summarize the way you live, or *want* to. This quiz should help you focus:

1. Is this room in the "public" part of the house where guests will be entertained? Is it the domain of one or two members of the household?

2. Will this room be used all the time? Once or twice a day? Infrequently, when guests come, or there's a special occasion?

3. Do you entertain frequently (several times a month)? Occasionally (once every month or so)? Infrequently (two or three times a year)?

4. Do you prefer formal entertaining (cocktails and sit-down dinners)? Less formal entertaining (cocktails and buffets)? Informal get-togethers (bridge, or refreshments and talk)?

5. What do you want in the room: art, collectibles, piano?

What mood do you want to establish?

As we've seen, each season has fairly predictable personality types that go with it. In the main, you can count on Winters to be dramatic, sometimes to the point of theatrics. Summers are calm and refined. Autumns are naturally easy and outgoing. Springs are whimsical, perhaps sophisticated, but always fun-loving. But within these broadbrush characterizations, there's plenty of room for individual personality types. Think about *yours*, and then decide which of two categories it comes closest to fitting: formal or less formal. Once you establish that, you begin to focus on the kind of furnishings you'll most enjoy living with, and consequently, what style of furniture you should buy. For instance, "country" is inherently informal, when you're talking about old mellow pine, and braided rugs on red brick floors. That's the perfect ambience for an Autumn. But translate "country" into black-painted comb-back Windsor chairs, and dramatic Amish quilts against stark white walls, and a Winter could live there elegantly ... and with a degree of formality.

Where do you live?
Where is your room actually located?
What style of architecture are you dealing with?

These are practical considerations, rather than arbiters of taste. Are you in a city apartment, suburban ranch, or in a sprawling, old country farmhouse? Your style need not be affected dramatically—we've seen charming little country retreats on the 17th floor of a New York condo—but location can dictate some practical decorating decisions. Would wall-to-wall carpeting really be a good idea where you walk right in from unpaved roads? Could you do *without* its acoustical advantages in a city apartment? Likewise, bare windows that are so wonderful when the view is, too, could be awful over-looking a brick wall. A lot of this is common sense, of course. We just thought we'd remind you.

Now, about the exact location of the room within your home. As we've pointed out, the quality of light in a room can, indeed, affect the colors you use. Nowadays, with most of us out of the house during the daytime, the light under discussion is usually artificial. If you're an exception, and your room will see plenty of use by daylight, then you should know that northern light is blue and cool, calling for even warmer hues (in the case of Autumns and Springs), and more intense colors (Winters and Summers). If your exposure is southern, you may want to compensate with even cooler colors (Winters and Summers), or with less intense warms (Autumns and Springs). Beyond that, a room's exposure has little effect on your decorating decisions.

Finally, the architecture within which you are creating your color scheme can play a major role in your decision-making. In the first place, it may influence the decorating style you choose, and therefore, the ultimate ambience you're out to create. For example, if you live in a center-hall colonial, you'd be going against its architectural grain to fill it with drop-dead contemporary. However, since we can't always choose the style of the building—especially true for apartment-dwellers—there are, happily, no rules against superimposing your personal style on any architecture.

Sleek contemporary can look smashing in traditional interiors, just as country can look sophisticated in open, contemporary rooms. What you generally need to make such crossovers work is a nod to the room's architectural style in the furnishings you choose for it. For instance, leaving the windows sleek and bare will make contemporary look more at-home in a traditional room.

However, you should generally let your architecture determine the type of scheme you're going to work out, using *your colors*.

- *Traditional rooms* lend themselves best to related and contrasting color schemes. Doubtless, that's because we're used to seeing them in multi-colors. However, all-white-plus-one-color can also be very traditional, especially when the color is blue. Highly formal traditional rooms can look quite elegant done in all-white or all-neutrals. Either provides the serene background to show off good art and antiques.

- *Contemporary rooms* are naturals for neutrals and all-white schemes. If you're out to make a definite, high-style decorating statement, go all-out with all-white. Nothing shows off art and sculpture more effectively.

- *Casual and informal rooms* seem to profit equally well from bright, multi-color schemes and from generous uses of neutrals. A beach house, for example, could be done in umbrella-brights, or in the natural colors of the beach itself (sand, grasses, driftwood).

Color Scheming with *Your Colors*

It's time to apply everything you've learned about color in general, and about *your colors* in specific.

Remember that there are four ways to set any color scheme:

- With colors that are in contrast to each other
- With colors that are related to each other
- With a range of neutrals, or "no-colors"
- With all-white-plus-one color

Any season can use any one of these formulas successfully, provided you stay with your own palette and use those colors that are most becoming to you. As you choose the colors you're going to be living with, remember that you will indeed be *living* with them, possibly for a long, long time. *All your colors* may be good for you to *wear* but some may lend themselves more easily to fashions for the home.

As you decide which of the four formulas to apply, consider this:

- *Contrasting schemes* should be cool and sharp for Winters, warm and bright for Springs. For Summers, the contrast should be cool and soft; for Autumns, warm and muted. In practice, this rule applies itself, as long as you use the colors in your palette.

- *Related schemes* are most successful when they involve no more than two colors, plus white, and perhaps an accent color.

- *Neutral schemes* need a variety in textures to keep them from looking too homogenized and bland.

- *All-white-plus-one-color schemes* work well for any season, as long as you use *your* white.

Contrasting color schemes

Contrasting color schemes are easy to borrow from fabrics or wallcovering patterns, where the colors are already established for you. If you can't find a starting pattern to follow, it's almost as easy to set your own scheme of contrasting colors. Just follow these three steps:

1. Choose your favorite color from your palette.

2. Look back and find it on the color wheel, page 42. The color that lies directly opposite that color on the wheel is its true complement.

3. Now find *your* version of that complement on your palette. It doesn't have to be a perfect match, as long as it is *cool* or *warm,* to match your season.

You may have noticed that we prefer the word *contrasting* to *complementary* (found in other decorating guides), because true complements might not be among your colors and, therefore, not the most flattering colors for you. Better to use *any* color that lies on the other side of the wheel in *contrast* to the color you're starting with. An example to show you how this kind of color adaptation works:

- Periwinkle, a blue-violet, is in everyone's palette. Its actual complement on the color wheel is yellow-orange, which is fine if you're an Autumn or Spring. But if you're a Winter or Summer, you should adjust that yellow-orange to the yellow that's included in your palette.

Related color schemes

Stealing colors from a ready-made source (such as fabric) can also work beautifully when you want to establish a room scheme around related colors.

If you want to set your own scheme, refer to the color wheel again. Remember, there are two ways to go about it. You can use colors that are monochromatic—various shades of the same color—or analogous—those near each other on the wheel.

Neutral color schemes

Neutral color schemes can provide beautiful backgrounds for *any season* in any room where you want to create an air of quiet and composure. Remember, however, that it's easy to slip into the *boring* category unless you have enough variety in the textures of the room's furnishings.

Winter's best textures have sparkle and shine ... mirrored walls and high-gloss lacquer; Summer's are softer but still "cool" to the eye ... fabrics with a light sheen and matte lacquer. Autumn's are the naturals ... warm woods and textured fabrics; for Springs, the textures should be both definite and delicate, such as woven wicker and polished cotton.

As you plan your neutral color scheme, pick furnishings and accessories for the way they will play against each other in the room. Avoid repeating textures that actually touch each other. For example, if your sofa is covered in velvet, use anything *but* a velvet-pile rug under it. You need the subtle difference in surface finishes to intrigue the eye and ward off boredom.

All-white-plus-one-color schemes

All-white-plus-one-color schemes let you choose *any* color from *your* palette to add to *your* white. That color may be used as accent only, or you can reverse the procedure and make *it* the dominant color, with white playing the supporting color role.

For example, use your favorite color from your palette on the walls and repeat it in an area rug, in pillows tossed on your upholstered pieces, and in the print of the fabric at your windows. Everything else should be white—woodwork, upholstery, and roman shades under your print draperies.

If you prefer a lighter background, let white dominate—on walls, woodwork, upholstery, and rug—and use the color in small touches on throw pillows, as a border on the rug, in the print of the fabric at the windows, even picked up and played back by important art in the room.

Your Decorating Colors, a Season-by-Season Guide

Color Schemes for <u>Winters</u>

Since the key word for Winters is dramatic, you literally sparkle in rooms with strong color contrasts. Your own coloring is so definite, you can hold your own—beautifully—against any color in your palette.

Contrasting color schemes for Winters let you bring in the brights in various intensities. Obviously, if you use colors at full strength, the contrast will be at its most intense. Depending on the ultimate effect you're out to achieve, you can adjust the intensities up and down the scale, changing the mood of the room as you go. For example, red and green are true complements that literally vibrate when they're used together at full intensity. If, however, you ice or darken either one (or both), you can come up with a variety of contrasting schemes based on red and green. Some terrific contrasting colors for Winters are:

- True Red and True Green
- True Green and True Purple
- True Purple and True Yellow
- True Yellow and True Blue
- True Blue and True Red
- True Red and True Yellow

All-white color schemes are obviously the easiest to create but they call for special attention to textures. Dark or glossy lacquered woods and sparkling accessories will give the room the contrast that sets a Winter off to best advantage.

All-white-plus-one-color schemes are excellent for Winters. Your cool snow-white looks even whiter when it comes up against any other vivid Winter color. Especially dynamic duos are:

- White and True Red
- White and True Green
- White and True Blue

- White and True Purple
- White and Icy Gray
- White and Black

All-white-plus-black-plus-one-color schemes are a dramatic extension of the all-white-plus . . . idea. They're so dramatic, in fact, that only a Winter's equally definite coloring can stand up to their sharp contrast. White-black-plus-one-color schemes are sensational in both updated traditional interiors and contemporary spaces. The one color you choose must be one that can hold its own against these polar opposites, black and white. Looking over Winter's palette, a number of candidates pop out: true yellow, turquoise, true green.

Related color schemes, as a rule, provide less visual excitement than a Winter usually needs for her environment to be most flattering. However, all that changes if you choose the right relatives. Some related colors for Winters are:

- Icy Pink and Strawberry Pink
- Icy Green and True Green
- Icy Violet and True Purple
- True Purple and Fuchsia
- Emerald Green and True Blue
- True Blue and True Purple

Neutral schemes can also have their share of the drama Winters need. A flattering background for a career woman in a city apartment with contemporary furniture would be icy taupe, an illusive color that changes with the light. Neutral schemes are naturals for Winter men since they lend themselves to tailored, masculine rooms. A city apartment would look handsome in "gray-flannel" gray. Some neutral combinations for Winters are:

- True Gray and Black
- Taupe and Black
- True Gray and Taupe

Color Schemes for Summers

Summers thrive in rooms where there is some contrast, but not the sharp, ringing contrast of Winters. Summers look their best against backgrounds that are slightly powdery and soft.

Contrasting color schemes for Summers call for soft versions of the primaries: the *red* is pink ... *yellow*, soft ... *blue*, powdery. The complements of these down-keyed colors will be equally gentled and cool, as you can see on your palette. For example, let's see how red and green can complement each other in Summer's color idiom. Downright dazzling used together in pure form, they must both be lightened and softened until the red is pink and the green is a mint green. They're still contrasting colors, but *now* they belong in a Summer's rooms. Some lovely contrasting colors for Summers are:

- Powder Pink and Mint Green
- Mint Green and Lilac
- Lilac and Soft Yellow
- Soft Yellow and Powder Blue
- Powder Blue and Powder Pink
- Powder Pink and Soft Yellow

All-white color schemes make attractive backgrounds for Summers when soft contrast is provided by light-to-medium ash-tone or matte lacquered woods and gentle variations in textures.

All-white-plus-one-color schemes are a somewhat more classic approach to basic white rooms. Any of the colors in your palette can be the other color. Even the softest Summer color can hold its own against your off-white. Some white-plus ideas for Summers include:

- Off-White and Lilac
- Off-White and Mint Green
- Off-White and Powder Pink
- Off-White and Powder Blue
- Off-White and Soft Aqua
- Off-White and Soft Periwinkle

Related color schemes are soft and quietly elegant, providing an altogether lovely setting for Summer's own coloring. Some good related colors for Summers are:

- Petal Pink and Rose Pink
- Lilac and Lavender
- Powder Blue and Sky Blue
- Powder Pink and Lilac
- Mint Green and Powder Blue
- Powder Blue and Lilac

Neutral color schemes can take great advantage of Summer's tender rose beiges and rose browns . . . or, of your gray-blues and grayed navy. A Summer man, for instance, would look well in any of these combinations:

- Rose Beige and Rose Brown
- Blue Gray and Gray Blue
- Rose Beige and Grayed Navy

Color Schemes for Autumns

Autumn's colors are earthy, warm, and muted, and tend to be natural and casual. Any one of the four color formulas can be used to translate that attitude into your rooms.

Contrasting color schemes for Autumns should be muted, whether the colors are dusty or clear. Those classic contrasting colors, red and green, come very naturally to Autumns. In your palette, the red is an orange-red and the green is sun-warmed with yellow. Used together at the deeper end of the color scale, they add up to rooms that are steeped in tradition. Lightened to peach and jade green, they create an entirely different contemporary mood. Some contrasting colors for Autumns are:

- Tangerine and Jade Green
- Jade Green and Orange
- Orange and Teal Blue
- Teal Blue and Gold
- Gold and Periwinkle
- Periwinkle and Orange

Related color schemes for Autumns are based on the same wonderful colors of Nature and work together just as naturally indoors to complement your own rich, warm coloring. Some related colors for Autumns are:

- Peach and Tangerine
- Aqua and Teal Blue
- Apricot and Orange
- Moss Green and Teal Blue
- Orange and Tangerine
- Gold and Avocado

All-white-plus-one-color schemes for Autumns naturally star your season's warm oyster white. You have a large supporting cast from which to choose the room's co-star. Any color in your palette will look good with oyster. Some white-plus schemes for Autumns are:

- Oyster and Moss Green
- Oyster and Turquoise
- Oyster and Orange
- Oyster and Teal Blue
- Oyster and Gold
- Oyster and Tangerine

Neutral schemes for Autumns are naturals, because you enjoy that certain muted warmth in all your colors. You can easily expand on the oyster-white theme by introducing other nearby neutrals such as warm beige and brown. Since the neutrals in the palette are naturally earthy and muted, there is a wide choice of color combinations for an Autumn man. Some neutral combinations for Autumns are:

- Warm Beige and Milk Chocolate
- Camel and Dark Chocolate
- Warm Beige and Coffee

Color Schemes for Springs

Springs present a pretty paradox. They are the most delicate of all the seasons, but they look best in rooms where the contrast is bright and crisp.

Contrasting color schemes for Springs play up the playful opposites in your palette. No dark or off-colors need apply. Spring's colors and their complements are as fresh and bright as the season itself. Look what happens to red and green when these contrasting colors are translated into Spring's palette: the red is a bright, warm pink and the green is a clear yellow-green. Together, they make a crisp yet delicate contrast that shows off a Spring in her element. Too much contrast could overwhelm a Spring's delicate coloring. Some contrasting colors for Spring are:

- Warm Pink and Spring Green
- Spring Green and Nectarine
- Nectarine and Sky Blue
- Sky Blue and Orange
- Orange and Periwinkle
- Periwinkle and Sunny Yellow

Related color schemes for Springs will have a sprightliness of their own since they will revolve around the crisp, bright colors in your palette. There's virtually no end to the color choices you can make as long as they're warm and clear. Some related colors for Springs are:

- Peach and Nectarine
- Lavender and Violet
- Shell Pink and Warm Pink
- Sky Blue and Violet
- Orange and Nectarine
- Spring Green and Turquoise

All-white-plus-one-color schemes for Springs work beautifully every time, and are still the easiest way of all to put a room together. The white here is actually ivory, warmed with yellow, and the perfect lead-in to Spring's clear, warm colors. Some white-plus schemes for Springs are:

- Ivory and Turquoise
- Ivory and Nectarine
- Ivory and Spring Green
- Ivory and Sky Blue
- Ivory and Orange
- Ivory and Periwinkle

All-white-plus-no-color-or neutral rooms can also be beautiful places for Springs to be. "No-color" is an exaggeration, of course; you'll get ample visual interest from woods, textures, and accessories. All-ivory works well in a contemporary room for Spring. For a Spring man's apartment, use the all-ivory formula but choose materials such as leather and brass for contrast. Some neutral combinations for Springs are:

- Light Camel and Clear Navy
- Warm Beige and Milk Chocolate
- Dove Gray and Clear Navy

Color Considerations for Others You Live With

The second question everyone asks about living with *your colors at home* is invariably:

> "What if the other people I live with belong to different
> seasons? What about my mate? My children?"

The answer has usually been implied in the first question people ask: "What's *my* season?" Chances are you're the woman of the house, and this is *your* territory you're coloring to make *you* look and feel terrific. Contemporary thinking has changed many of our attitudes and expectations, especially on the home front, but the domestic scene still belongs to the female half of the team. The bad news is that most domestic chores still end up in our laps, too. But then that more than earns you the right to consider *your* season first when mapping out decorating plans.

If you still feel guilt twinges, try this little exercise:

- Do you frequently (twice a month) entertain his business associates or friends?

- Do you usually answer the door and greet your guests?

- Does he frequently notice and comment on what you're wearing when you're home alone?

- Does he have his own territory in the house, such as a study, home office, or dressing room/bath?

If you've answered "yes" at least three times, then your conscience should be clear. This man you live with has every reason to want *you* to be the star of the home show. He's proud of your looks and will enjoy seeing you at your best, surrounded by the colors that are most flattering to *you*. If you could answer "yes" to the last question, then your only obligation is to make the most of his palette when you do over *his* private spaces.

Having said all that, however, you may be relieved to know that there is a handful of season-spanning colors that can be flattering to everyone:

- Aqua
- Periwinkle
- Coral Pink

Almost everyone looks good in schemes based on one of these colors, especially when they're liberally laced with white. Whose white? Probably the all-around best compromise between seasons is the off-white of Summer.

For more variety in planning season-spanning schemes, study the palette of everyone involved, looking for colors that come fairly close to each other. Winters and Summers sharing quarters have a fairly easy time of it, since both seasons are based on cool colors with blue undertones. Ditto for Springs and Autumns who are decorating in tandem; they both look best in warm colors with yellow undertones.

It's when a cool palette must co-exist with a warm palette that the color wars begin. Our advice: reach for Summer's off-white. It offers the best way around the season mix. Use it to create rooms that are basically all-white and merely accented with one or two of the colors you do have in common.

Children pose much less of a problem than spouses. Since they're a combination of you both, they usually fall into one season or the other. But sometimes they can introduce a third season. In this case, opt for the season-spanners, or use off-white and accents you all enjoy for the public areas of the house. You can each indulge your palette in your personal spaces. And, what about siblings who share a room but not a season? Aqua and white are bright and cheerful and appropriate for either sex.

A final hint to you still-single women: solve the whole issue up-front and marry someone of your own season. It's one thing you'll always have in common, and your lifetime of decorating decisions will be much easier.

CHAPTER IV

What's Your Style?

Furniture offers a virtually endless choice of styles. But, like color, some of those styles are better suited to your particular personality and your way of life. There's nothing new about that, of course. You can literally read the history of humankind in the furniture designed and built for our homes down through the years. The Romans had their dining chaises, Napoleonic France, its Empire furniture; the English developed the tea table for the service of their newly discovered passion in the 18th century, and today, we've turned it into the coffee table that's perhaps more reflective of our times.

That's part of what makes this whole business of interior design both a fine art and a fun art. But it's also a highly subjective art form, especially when it comes to choosing furniture. It's mainly a matter of your tastes and preferences, and the good news is, if you really love a certain style or piece of furniture, you can have it. Unlike color, there's no really *wrong* style of furniture for you, as long as you use it in an environment filled with your best colors. However, there *are* some furniture styles that promise to be more compatible than others with the different seasons' personalities. And there are definitely wood tones and finishes that are especially flattering for each.

What's Your Style—A Season-by-Season Guide

Winter

Furniture styles for Winters focus on the formal and the grand, with dark woods and lacquered finishes. A canopy bed … regal Chippendale secretary or tall chest … contemporary glass table on a sculptured chrome base … the *avant garde* in sofa designs. This is furniture that makes a very definite statement.

Of course, there are many kinds of personalities behind that Winter coloring, so if you love country furniture, go ahead and have it. But don't try to make it down-home country. It's just not *you*. What is, as we mentioned earlier, could be country couched in the sophisticated silhouette of black-painted Windsor chairs or a grandfather clock.

Of all the seasons, Winters have the widest choice of furniture styles. Virtually every period can be terrific in your rooms, as long as you keep remembering these three key Winter words:

1. *Dramatic.* Even such familiar traditional pieces as a Hepplewhite wing chair are dramatic in styling and scale.

2. *Contrasting.* Dark woods and finishes give a Winter's rooms the definition they need.

3. *Sparkle.* High-gloss finishes and sparkling materials such as lacquered woods, glass, and gleaming metals are important.

Some furniture styles that are best in a Winter's rooms include:

- Formal 18th- and 19th-century traditional English and American: Chippendale, Hepplewhite, Sheraton, Regency, Duncan Phyfe, some Victorian, and the larger, more dramatic Country English pieces
- Classic French: Louis XVI and Empire
- Oriental
- Mission
- Art Deco
- Neoclassic
- Contemporary: the classics and the experimentally new

**Prints and Patterns
for Winters**

Winters should look for silky, shiny finishes that are both refined and elegant. This moire stripe is an excellent choice.

More important, perhaps, than the style of furniture a Winter chooses is the color of its wood and the way its surface is finished. Ideal for Winters are:

- Mahogany
- Walnut
- Oak
- Ebony
- Rattan
  (All the above in dark brown)
- Wrought iron in white, black, or dark green
- Lacquered or painted woods or laminates in white or black, the neutrals, or such brights as red, blue, and green
- Wood finishes that are highly polished
- Lacquered, painted, and metal surfaces that shine

Wallcoverings for Winters provide the backdrop for the drama we've come to expect of your season. No wallflowers for you, and we mean that literally! Select prints that are sharp, bold, and stylized, rather than realistic. You can stand up to the contrast; let it provide the perfect stage set to make you the star.

The texture of your walls should add to the overall sparkle of your rooms. Choose fabrics that are glazed, use high-gloss paints and lacquered finishes, and if it fits your overall theme, mirror-like foil wallcoverings are good. So, of course, are mirror panels, especially with edges beveled to enhance their gleam. A Winter with formal, traditional tastes will look regal against walls of dark, Georgian-style wood paneling.

Flooring styles for Winters set the pace for sophisticated furnishings to come. Wood is the perfect way to underscore any room, and Winters should have it stained deep and dark, polished almost to a glitter. Conversely, a floor bleached or painted white will really set off your furniture, whether it's contemporary or traditional. Of all the seasons, Winters can best leave floors totally naked, beautiful in their simplicity.

Other good choices in hard-surface floors for Winters' rooms include highly glazed ceramic tiles, and the resilients in strong, solid colors. White or black marble would be terrific in a foyer. Use both in a classic checkerboard pattern for the utmost in drama.

Floorcoverings for Winters should provide sharp spots of color, or contrast boldly with the flooring beneath. Among the area rugs that will do the trick are geometric patterns, kilims in vivid colors, and needlepoint rugs with a black background.

Floorcloths will work equally well in country or informal, traditional rooms, and in a contemporary setting. So will kilims in your boldest colors. For a more formal look, an Oriental is excellent; it should be strong in color and pattern. Wall-to-wall carpeting can be luxurious velvet pile, or it can have a sculptured pile surface.

Prints and Patterns for Winters

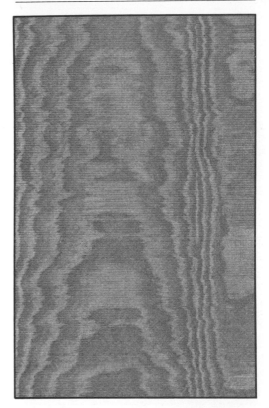

Most patterns . . . checks, plaids, and stripes . . . are too formal for Winters. This stylized moire offers Winters another formal option in fabrics and wallcoverings.

Window styles for Winters can be grandiloquent, or severely tailored. In between, of course, you have as many options as you need to suit the style of your room. Especially good for you are definite, hard-edged shapes, such as upholstered or painted cornices and lambrequins. While all seasons can use vertical or miniblinds, only Winters should have them with the new mirrored or bright silver-metallic finishes.

Fabric styles for Winters should include silks and satins. They are excellent choices since they have the surface shine that is so right for you. So do metallicized leathers, and fabrics with silver or colored metallic threads woven in. Brocades, velvets, damasks, failles, taffetas, and moires are also extremely flattering.

Accessories for Winters should provide the final touch of sparkle and shine to round out the theme you've set for yourself. Crystal is a perfect medium— in a chandelier, a collection of paperweights, flower vases. Acrylic adds the same kind of sparkle to more contemporary rooms, and you can find it in everything from small boxes to cube tables and works of sculpture. Little mirrored things are marvelous, of course. Your metal is silver-toned. Opt for it in fireplace accessories, candlesticks, picture frames, and desk accessories. Oriental *objets* are also perfect. A coromandel screen would be dynamite behind a sofa or in a dining room. Chinese porcelains, cloisonne boxes with their jewel-like colors, even a kimono in brilliant silks and embroidery could become an arresting work of wall art, worthy of a Winter's room.

Flowers for Winters are the most dramatic in nature's repertoire: long stemmed roses or sculptured lilies for your crystal vases; azalea and poinsettia plants.

Summer

Furniture styles for Summers revolve around the classics from design history past, focusing on the periods that are formal, yes, but less dramatic than Winters'. Summers get elegant Queen Anne, with its soft lines and gracefully curving cabriole legs, as interpreted in both 18th-century England and America.

The same difference applies to French styling, which is ideal for most Summers. While the periods now known as Louis XVI and Empire are right down a Winter's alley with their strong shapes and dramatic lines, a Summer's softer nature is best expressed in the elegantly feminine styling of the Louis XV period. Overall, a Summer's look in furniture can be summed up in three key words:

1. *Classic.* The furnishings are well-bred, and the ambience is one of unstudied, easy elegance.
2. *Correct.* Summers are too refined to deal in the whimsical or experimental.
3. *Soft.* Both the silhouettes and wood colors of a Summer's furniture are soft, never dramatic or harsh.

Some of the furniture styles that are best for Summers include:

- Classic 18th- and 19th-century traditional English and American, especially Queen Anne; some of the simpler Chippendale styles; some American Country, such as the graceful bowback Windsor chair
- Classic French: Louis XV, both the more elegant "Court" styles, and the simpler, country-made copies
- Contemporary: soft and curvy

The colors of the woods and finishes of a Summer's furniture should be as softly refined as the season itself. Perfect are:

- Mahogany
- Walnut
- Maple
- Ash
- Beech
- Birch

(All the above in light ash blonde to medium ash brown)

**Prints and Patterns
for Summers**

Summers thrive in all-over patterns that could have been taken from a Monet painting. In this blended rose floral, no one color dominates the design.

- Wrought iron, painted off-white
- Wicker, painted off-white
- Painted woods that have been antiqued or distressed to produce a soft patina. They can be off-white, a neutral, or painted in one of your light colors: powder blue, soft yellow, or powder pink
- Low-gloss is the word for the finishes on both woods and painted surfaces

Wallcoverings for Summers should revolve around patterns that are soft and blended, with no one color dominating the design. Think of watercolor paintings or pastel drawings, where the colors meld gently into each other. Florals and realistic motifs are good—you can also use calm geometric designs, such as stripes, and plaids, as long as they are blended and subtle.

Surface textures should be equally soft. If paint is your medium, use one that dries to a flat or eggshell surface. Classic wood paneling is another wall treatment for a Summer's formal rooms. For you, paneling carved in the curved style of the Louis XV period would be perfect, and it's available, inexpensively, for do-it-your-self installations. Bleach it, or paint it your off-white, or use a stain in the ash tone that's most becoming to your season.

Flooring styles for Summers should be so soft and muted that the floor itself never really commands that much attention. Rather, it blends into the overall calm, classic scheme that shows *you* off to best advantage.

Wood floors for Summers should be stained either ash blonde or ash brown. Or, for a lovely change of pace in less-formal or contemporary rooms, consider painting your wood floor off-white or a pastel from your palette.

If you opt for any of the other hard-surface flooring materials, your best looks include off-white toned marble and ceramic tiles with a gentle surface luster.

Floorcoverings for Summers should underscore the elegant ambience of the rest of the room's furnishings. Everything we just said about patterns in your wallcoverings applies to what you put on your floors, as well. Patterns should be gently blended so no one color or motif asserts itself. Florals in tender pastels are perfect for traditional rooms where you want a more formal mood. Where the attitude's more relaxed and informal—in a country-style room, say—rag rugs in pastels would be an update of a time-honored idea.

For contemporary and eclectic rooms, consider a dhurrie in one of your neutrals, or a velvet pile wall-to-wall carpet in a neutral or your off-white.

Prints and Patterns for Summers

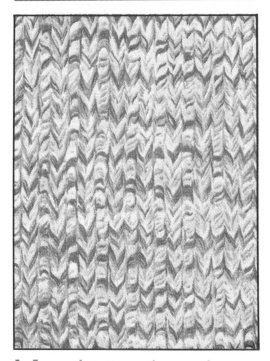

In Summer's patterns, the general impression is one of softness, color, and light. This blended watercolor is a fine example of Summer's soft look.

Window styles for Summers take us, as usual, to gentled versions of the ideas already outlined for Winters, plus a few new Summer-soft suggestions. Summers can enjoy the currently popular balloon shades that work so well with classic, antique-filled rooms.

For more casual members of the Summer season, there are wood-louvered shutters, or wood shutters shaped with a French flavor and filled with gathered fabric. Either way, the wood can be painted off-white, or to match the color of the wall.

Fabric styles for Summers follow the same trend we've already set for your walls and floors. Patterns should be blended, gentle, and soft-spoken, and surface textures rich, but quietly so. Start with the ubiquitous velvets. Add subtle woven cottons and blends, linens with a soft hand and texture, and raw silks with a slightly slubbed surface. Choose leathers with just a whisper of a surface shine, and your suedes, if any, should be Ultra.

Accessories for Summers include the classics. Impressionist-style paintings and prints are perfect examples, with their soft colors and brushstrokes. While we're in this classic French mood, add faience, porcelain, and tole *objets* to your best accessories list, too.

Cool and classic itself, marble is a marvelous addition to a Summer's rooms. Make it off-white, and have it in ashtrays, plant stands, and lamp bases. Mother of pearl is another natural, quite literally speaking, for you to collect and display. Summer's best metals are silver-toned or rose-gold. Fireplace tools and other accessories, any metallic touches on furniture and lamps should be cast in these flattering finishes. On the soft side of the accessory picture for Summers: a collection of throw pillows on a sofa or bed, all in slubbed silks, velvets, and petitpoint.

Flowers for Summers come right off your palette: lilacs and irises in your cool blues and roses and glads in your flattering pinks; painted daisies for country rooms.

Autumn

Furniture styles for Autumns also have an heirloom quality about them, but in a rather different mood from Summers'. The provenance of Autumn's furniture is primarily Old England in the era of the grand country manor . . . robust rather than refined . . . sportive, comfortable, and relaxed, yet with an easy-going dignity that says you have nothing to prove. Think of wing chairs with high, embracing backs and turned stretchers . . . of oak hunt tables and William & Mary-style sideboards. Much of America's 17th- and early 18th-century country furniture is perfect for your rooms since it was made by emigrant artisans who were still imitating the fashionable styles they had left behind.

Translated into contemporary terms, an Autumn's furniture is comfortable and conducive to put-your-feet-up, easy living. No drop-dead styling, no company manners required! Everyone feels welcome and at home with Autumn's furniture. If there are three key words to keep in mind as you collect the furnishings for your rooms, they'd have to be:

1. *Natural.* For all their rich design heritage, the furniture that best suits Autumns is very down-to-earth and welcoming.

2. *Comfortable.* Physically, as well as emotionally, the furniture is meant for easy living by outdoorsy, nature-loving people.

3. *Mellow.* It follows that the colors of the woods and any painted finishes will be in warm browns, or from the sunshine side of the color wheel.

Some of the furniture styles that are best for Autumns are:

- 17th- and 18th-century English and American pieces, especially William & Mary and the simpler Chippendale and Queen Anne styles, and such Country English pieces as a Welsh cupboard and Windsor chairs

- Contemporary: comfortably scaled

- Scandinavian Modern

Prints and Patterns for Autumns

Autumns can use all types of textures, from twills to crackled leather and suedes. Among Autumn's best looks is this textured country linen.

The colors of the woods and finishes most suitable for Autumns are in the medium-to-dark range, although some golden brown pine is appropriate in American country pieces. Best for Autumns are:

- Cherry
- Maple
- Pine
- Mahogany
- Oak
- Teak
- Walnut (All the above in medium-to-dark brown)
- Wicker, natural or stained
- Painted woods that have a low-gloss finish, or are antiqued and distressed for a more muted finish. Oyster-white, neutrals, and medium-to-dark colors such as gold, teal blue, and orange are good for occasional pieces
- Wood finishes should also be low-gloss

Wallcoverings for Autumns should be self-assured but never extroverted. By that, we mean the best type of pattern for your walls is one that is strong enough to be noticed, but never dominates the overall room. The general feeling is blended, rather than sharp, which befits a season whose colors blend very naturally anyway. Some especially good patterns for you include paisleys, plaids, and stripes.

Autumns can indulge in the most exciting textures of all the seasons. Your options range all the way from burlap and twill-surfaced wallcoverings, to stucco and natural brick. If you elect to paint your walls, use flat-finish paint, with semi-gloss on the trim. And if you choose to panel your walls, consider paneling stained the medium-to-dark brown that goes so well with you and with the vintage country-manor look that suits your season so well.

Flooring styles for Autumns are quite literally the basis upon which your natural-looking or heritage-rich rooms are founded. In this category are flooring materials that give your rooms a pleasing interplay of textures: brick, quarry tile, and wood. Your penchant for things Old English makes wood flooring a "natural" in more traditional rooms, too. Wide-planked, pegged oak floors are perfect, stained a medium-to-dark, rich brown. Autumns can also enjoy painted floors. Try oyster white under contemporary furnishings, or experiment with one of the special paint effects, interpreted in your darker, warm colors.

Floorcoverings for Autumns should be rich with the textures that come naturally to your outdoorsy, easy-living rooms. Nothing precious, nothing fastidious allowed here. Honest textures, natural materials, and a relax-and-feel welcome attitude in your rooms dictate floors covered in sturdy stuff. Sisal matting, braided rugs, handmade Berbers, and American Indian rugs, with their autumnal colors and straightforward designs, are among the ideal choices for area rugs in less formal rooms. Where the ambience is more traditional, patterned rugs in muted colors are a good solution. Wall-to-wall carpeting also has a place and can be equally effective in contemporary or traditional settings. A velvet

Prints and Patterns for Autumns

Patterns that are subtle and muted are best for Autumn's easygoing rooms. This linen stripe would be a good choice, with its blended colors and natural, textured surface.

pile carpet is good, but better, especially where the mood's contemporary, would be tweedy or textured wall-to-wall.

Window styles for Autumns should carry forth your warm, comfortable, perhaps English theme. And when it comes to dressing windows with such a heritage, almost any of the traditional treatments will work, as long as you interpret them in *your* fabric textures, in woods, or even in stained glass. If you lack the real thing, you can achieve the same effect by hanging a wood-framed panel of stained glass over an ordinary window.

Since Autumn's rooms are both natural and traditional in outlook, wood is an inherently appropriate medium for your window treatments. Consider wooden Venetian blinds, one of the newer miniblinds, or louvered shutters. To complement the other woods in your rooms, stain them medium-to-dark brown.

Fabric styles for Autumns should meet the same criteria when it comes to prints and patterns as wallcoverings: definite but not bold. Blended, allover patterns, such as paisleys, plaids, and stripes, are good.

Your best look is in woven fabrics. For you, there's a wonderful range, from twills, chevrons, and herringbones, to blends that have an outright tweedy, tactile surface. Your leathers can be creased and crackled, your suedes as rich as rawhide. Of all the seasons, you can have the most variety in the velvets you use, but do avoid anything with a long, crushed pile. It's ugly, and *out*.

Accessories for Autumns should be warmly traditional, giving you centuries worth of treasures to draw from, in both the Old World and the New. Think of old leather-bound books, an antique globe, walls hung with Audubon prints, and you begin to get the picture. Everything in your rooms should be drawn from nature, and be made of natural materials: wood, leather, and earthenware pottery—this is your look. Your best metal is antiqued brass, so use it for fireplace accessories, candlesticks, and other small *objets* to reflect your glowing Autumn coloring—and personality.

Flowers for Autumns come in *your* colors and bloom in *your* season: mums, marigolds, asters, and zinnias; yellow daisies, straw flowers, and wheat for country rooms.

Spring

Furniture styles for Springs include everything delicate, whimsical, and sophisticated in the legacy of furniture, past and present. Whatever your personal taste, there's a style to express it, in perfect harmony with the best looks for Springs.

Your options range all the way from graceful Louis XV, with its delicate lines, to Victorian's curvy and charming style evocative of yesteryear's front parlor. In between, you can express your individual style in terms of feminine Queen Anne chairs and tables with long, sensuous, curving lines ... of handmade styles from the American countryside and the provinces of 18th-century France ... and contemporary pieces that are light in scale.

With so many choices on your plate, decoratively speaking, these three buywords are important to remember:

1. *Delicate.* Not for Springs, the heavily carved, the massive, the solid in bulk, or the stolid in spirit. Springs need furniture that's as fresh and vivacious in looks *and* outlook as they are.

2. *Sophisticated.* If Springs were a less fun-loving personality type, we'd say "elegant." But Springs can be sophisticated and self-assured enough to make that extra gesture, to express a personal quirk.

3. *Bright.* The woods and painted finishes best-suited to Springs come from the lighter end of the warm color spectrum.

Some of the furniture styles that are especially good for a Spring's habitat include:

- Classic Louis XV and the more lightly scaled Country French interpretations
- 18th- and 19th-century English and American styles in their more delicate versions, especially Queen Anne, Chippendale, and American Country
- Victorian
- Contemporary: light in scale

**Prints and Patterns
for Springs**

Remember the blended floral prints of Summer? Note that every Spring flower shown is clear and crisp against a plain background. The animated Spring pattern shown here is typical of this season's best look.

A Spring's best furniture woods are:

- Ash
- Beech
- Birch
- Mahogany
- Walnut
- Maple
- Pine
- Pecan

(All the above in light golden-blonde to medium golden-brown)

- Wrought iron, painted ivory
- Wicker, painted ivory
- Painted woods with a semi-gloss finish should be ivory or a bright color, such as sky blue, orange, or periwinkle
- Wood finishes should also be semi-gloss

Wallcoverings for Springs should be bright and perky, with animated prints and colors that fairly pop from the background. Choose patterns that are bright and crisp, but remember, you don't want to be overwhelmed by your own surroundings. Florals that are outlined for extra punch, and small, bright stripes are perfect. So is wallcovering with a crisp texture and finish, such as fine linen.

Painted walls could have a flat finish; use a semi-gloss paint on the trim. Or, you can use semi-gloss overall to give your walls the merest whisper of polish.

Flooring styles for Springs should provide the bright color foundation upon which the rest of the room depends. For you, spatter painting can be an ideal medium. It's a nice, almost gossamer visual surprise that would work equally well under American Country furnishings, with Victorian wicker, or with less formal contemporary. So would stenciled floors.

More sophisticated Springs could paint their floors ivory and have them lightly lacquered, or stain them a golden blonde or golden brown. Other good choices in hard-surface flooring would be ceramic tiles with a warm gloss, and resilients with bright designs.

Floorcoverings for Springs must also be bright and crisp. Smooth velvet-pile rugs and wall-to-wall carpeting are tailor-made for your rooms, whether they are sophisticated or charmingly nostalgic. For the former, think of Chinese silk rugs, with sculptured surface designs and bright, clear colors. Or, of patterned rugs and carpets scattered with flowers in the same crisp color-notes.

For a Spring in a nostalgic-romantic frame of mind, handloomed rag rugs in your brights would be perfect. Or, consider a slick, painted floorcloth. Depending on their design, this wonderful old idea in floorcoverings can look fresh and new for contemporary rooms, too.

Prints and Patterns for Springs

Spring's best patterns are crisp and sprightly so they practically 'pop' from the background. The perky print is exactly right for a Spring's fresh, bright rooms.

Window styles for Springs should be as open and airy as the season itself. Opt for the gossamer or the light, in both the fabrics and styles you choose. Eyelet and openwork lace are perfect for romantic-natured Springs. But if you sway to the more sophisticated side, a swag and jabot over sheer curtains is beautiful with Queen Anne furniture, or in a room inhabited by graceful Louis XV pieces.

Fabric styles for Springs are everything gossamer, delicate, and fine. Your linens should be smooth, cottons finely woven and lightly glazed, and your curtains made of lace, dimity, and other sheers. Silks for Springs are sophisticated and crisp. And if you include any leathers at all, they should be supple and beautifully polished.

Accessories for Springs should be as fresh and lively as the rest of the room's colors and furnishings. Watercolors and works of art in bright acrylics set the tone. If you're a collector, focus on porcelains, shells, cameos, and the like. For your less formal rooms, paint wicker baskets ivory and fill them with brilliant flowers. Also good for you are such feminine touches as romantic pillows, lace-trimmed and ruffled. Have a wealth of them in your boudoir. The best metal for Springs is polished brass. Use it for fireplace tools and accessories, and for candle holders filled with ivory tapers.

Flowers for Springs are just what you'd expect: lilies-of-the-valley, baby's breath, carnations, narcissus, sweetheart roses and violets; daisies for country rooms.

Your Style at a Glance

Chances are, you've been nodding "yes, yes" as you've read over the decorating basics that add up to the best decorating looks for your season. Perhaps you've *always* leaned toward the right choices, even if you're just discovering the seasonal theory for the first time. Be assured, you *will* eventually recognize your best looks instinctively and confidently. Until then, here's a thumbnail summary of what's right for your season.

Winter

Dark woods
Painted and lacquered woods
Lacquered or glazed walls
Dark-stained or painted floors
Oriental rugs
Shiny or silky fabrics
Stylized motifs
Silver-tone metals

Autumn

Medium-to-dark woods
Painted and antiqued woods
Matte-finish walls
Brick, quarry tile, or plank floors
Braided rugs
Textured fabrics
Natural motifs
Antique brass

Summer

Light-to-medium woods
Painted and antiqued woods
Matte-finish walls
Ash tone or painted floors
Floral pattern rugs
Fabrics with a soft sheen
Blended floral motifs
Silvertone or rose-gold metals

Spring

Light-to-medium woods
Painted and lightly lacquered woods
Semi-gloss walls
Painted or stenciled floors
Scattered floral pattern rugs
Fabrics with a bright sheen
Animated floral motifs
Polished brass

CHAPTER V

Your Colors—
All Around The House

Decorating is a visual art.

Words put down in black and white can only tell you what's in a room, and why. There's no way to convey the net result, the overall pleasure, of spaces made beautiful and livable with furnishings that have personality, and colors that are alive. You have to *see* for yourself.

That's what this section is all about. In it, you'll find rooms that show what you can do, using *your colors* from your season's palette.

Study all the rooms in this section, even if they best illustrate environments for seasons other than your own. They will help you understand what the different colors can do, why certain decorating decisions are made, and how any room comes together beautifully in the final analysis. As we've already stressed, interior decorating is a fine

art—a fun art—and a science, as well. Everyone must practice it from time to time. And now that you know *your colors* and how to use them, decorating should be more than a sometimes thing. Your home should always be evolving, changing, responding to changes in your attitude, your needs, and your way of living.

In fact, your palette is the one constant fact of your decorating life. It will never change because your own skin tones won't. What you buy today will always be *your color*, always right in your rooms. Secure in this knowledge, you're now free to indulge in both investment decorating—purchases that will justify their initial costs over the years to come—and in impulse-buying—lightweight purchases that may be passing fancies, but are fun for a while. The former give your rooms substance and

you, satisfaction; the latter help keep things fresh-looking and up-to-date. Since *home* reflects influences from the outside world, as well as inner stability, both are essential ingredients in any successful decorative scheme.

The parade of rooms that begins here includes just a sampling of all the color options and combinations available to you. Because everyone's home is such a personal place, you'll want to find your own way to successful rooms created around *your colors* and the furniture styles that set *you* off to best advantage.

Winter

Designer Lisa Rose of Aubergine Interiors, New York City, creates what she calls
a "quicksilver" background in a city apartment sleeked with cool neutrals.
A Winter would stand out dramatically against these icy gray walls,
which are highlighted by the almost theatrical recessed spotlighting.
Also very much in the Winter idiom:
the crystalline arch of the cocktail table . . . touches of the Orient in the accessories . . .
the chrome-based dining table, and the wall of sparkling, faceted mirrors.

Winter's Rooms are Dramatic

The Winter room is always an exciting place to be, as stimulating to the eye as it is to the psyche. *Contrast* is of the essence; the dark of Winter's woods against your brilliant white, and true, blue, clarion colors. Surfaces sparkle and gleam...each piece of furniture is self-important. No wall flowers here, figuratively or literally, since Winters generally shun floral patterns in favor of sharp-edged geometrics, dynamic solids, and dramatic textures. The exception would be an exceptional floral pattern indeed, and as sharply defined as a Winter's own coloring.

A contemporary setting for a Winter who loves traditional furniture: the all-white background is counterpointed by the dark mahogany of the dining table base, Chippendale chairs, and tall bookcases. Stained dark to emphasize the vertical interest they give the high-ceilinged room, the cases are painted inside to match the blue that wraps the wing chairs.

Putting drama down in black and white, designer Tanny Farah turns ordinary city apartment space, into an extra-ordinary bedroom background for a Winter woman. Mirrors, chrome, moulded acrylic, brilliant patent leather, and lacquered furniture meet Winters' needs for slick, shine, and sharp contrast in decorating. Of all the seasons, only Winter can stand up against such polar opposites as black and white.

All sparkle and shine, this is a setting to enhance a soft dramatic Winter with blue eyes and a taste for formal, traditional furniture. Restating the blue in the Oriental rug and at the arched window, the walls are lacquered to pick up the sparkle of the crystal chandeliers. Fabrics are silken; wood pieces are dark, gleaming mahogany.

Summer's Rooms are Classics

The word *soft* sums up the Summer room. Your white is gentled without losing its cool. Colors tend to the blue side of the spectrum, powdered and softened to create an essentially feminine background for furnishings that are equally refined. Only the impeccably tasteful will do for you. No extroverts allowed in Summer's natural habitat. You are quietly—but completely—in control, and your interiors say so, elegantly and irrefutably. Your rooms are somewhat formal and your furniture is classic and soft in silhouette, whether your taste is contemporary or traditional. Best for you are blended floral and watercolor patterns, textures that are subtle and elegant, genteel contrasts between colors and surfaces, and above all, an air of calm that reflects both your coloring and your temperament.

Summer's soft pastels whisper 'country' with an elegant accent in an inviting living room, *left*, designed by Carolyn Guttilla. This is country that's far from rustic, however. Summer's powder pink and a hint of powder blue in both the wallcovering and the subtle dhurrie rug are played against your soft off-white in a most genteel manner. This is country refined and recolored, so it reflects Summer's unique personality and coloring in the most flattering fashion. Any of Summer's contrasting colors will work beautifully with powder pink. Try soft yellow.

Photo: Wallcovering Information Bureau

97

Photo: Murray Hill Square, New Jersey

At left: An interesting, eclectic mix of styles and materials makes this mostly pink-and-white room a perfect setting for a Summer. Off-white ceramic tile floors and painted walls contrast tenderly with your related pinks and show off antiques and contemporary artworks with equal aplomb. It's practically impossible to make a decorating mistake when you start with your white as background and introduce only one or two colors into the scheme. Any of Summer's related colors will do beautifully. Remember that accessories, woods, and textures will provide additional visual excitement.

Above: Pink is pure flattery for a Summer, and can be teamed with an interesting variety of other colors from your palette. Here, it's mint green, leavened with generous amounts of Summer's off-white for a classic, sophisticated, eclectic living room in a renovated townhouse. Although what you see *above* is technically a contrasting color scheme, it has been softened and refined to flatter a Summer's own skin tones. Another contrasting color scheme could be built around Summer's lilac and mint green. For an even more appropriate Summer setting, the contrast between the woods and furniture in the room could be gentled and downplayed.

99

Autumn

Autumn's Rooms are Naturals

Natural is the key word for an Autumn's interiors. You look your very best in backgrounds that include rich, deep, warm colors, and furnishings that stand in muted contrast to each other. Nothing synthetic or showy allowed! You are a natural, indeed, and look and *feel* your very best in rooms filled with furniture that's totally unpretentious, comfortable, welcoming. Matte finishes become you; slick and shine might overwhelm your own natural coloring. Autumns should surround themselves with the products of the earth: warm, mellow woods, brick, quarry tile, stucco, and earthenware pottery. Just follow your own instincts—they'll lead you to create rooms where everyone feels at home, and *you* look your very best.

The serendipitous touch of jade green brightens an all-in-one kitchen/family/dining room for an Autumn, *above.* Aside from the natural ingredients—the flooring and barnside paneling—the color scheme revolves around one of Autumn's most becoming colors, red-orange. The two tones of jade come as a delightful surprise to the eye, enlivening the overall mood of the room. Teal blue is another color that would contrast well with red-orange. Typical of an Autumn's natural habitat, this is a room everyone loves to come home to, and relax in.

Photo: Thomasville Furniture Industries

Even in a city apartment, Autumns' best rooms look to the manor-born.
Here, the deep, warm brown woods of traditional style furniture work well
with the oyster white couch, golden tan walls, and touches of spicy orange.
More Autumn-oriented touches: the leather couch, handsome old leather-bound books,
and softly gleaming accents of brass.

Spring

Photo: Tom Yee

When Spring colors the country, it's as clear and fresh as
this bedroom drenched in blue, aqua, and turquoise, touched
with Spring's violet and peach on the bed. Since we didn't say
which country, the clean-limbed, light wood furniture could
claim either American Shaker or Scandinavian background. But
the overall look of the room itself—warm and bright—is
definitely the stuff of which stunning Spring settings are made!

Spring's Rooms are Bright

Spring's rooms have a way of always feeling brand-new and fresh, as if the colors have just been washed by April showers to make everything bright, clean, and clear. That's partly because Spring's palette is alive with such colors, of course, and partly because Spring herself is so vivacicus. You radiate in rooms where things are going on—where the furniture has personality, the fabrics are animated, the brass shines, and even the flowers are about to peak. Avoid the weighty, the massive, the dark. Dress your rooms as you would yourself—in colors that sing and patterns that 'pop.' Choose furniture that tends toward the light end of the spectrum, both in wood color and in styling. In fact, anything that goes into your background should have a *lilting* quality that reflects your own delicate coloring and effervescent personality.

Aqua warms the walls of a townhouse sitting room that's designed to be flattering to any Spring. Against such a bright background, almost every color from your palette will 'pop' attractively. Here, the choices are Spring green and ivory, with touches of peach in the pillows, picked up by the light orange Parsons table out in the hall. At the windows, curtains with a heading of ribbon repeat the color of the walls. The same ivory and aqua print covers the small screen that affords privacy during the day, when the curtains are open to the city streets. For a delightful variation on these colors, you might paint the walls peach or apricot, and use the aqua and Spring green as accents.

Photo: Celanese House

103

White Spans the Seasons in a Room for the Entire Family

Since family rooms are just that—rooms in which the whole family gathers—neutrals are natural choices for a color scheme that flatters everyone. This open, airy family room is white-washed liberally with off-white, a good choice when you're decorating to suit all seasons. There's enough variety in textures, so the only other color the room needs is supplied by such naturals as the wreaths, indoor plants and scenic view through the generous windows. You could introduce just one other color into such an all-white setting, if you wish.

And if using mostly white is too fragile for the way your family lives, try a mix of other neutrals.

Photo: JACK DONOHUE

CHAPTER VI

Backbone Decorating Information

This is the nitty-gritty decorating information that will help you put your rooms together confidently with the knowledge of what you're using, and why.

First, we walk you through the major rooms in your home, analyzing the traditional function of each and *re*thinking the space in light of today's changing lifestyles and your new approach to color.

Then, we get down to the hard facts: quickstudies of all the ingredients that make up a successfully decorated room. Don't leave home without this ready reference when you set out to buy for your decorating projects. Not only will you be able to speak the language when you're talking with the salesperson, you'll know what you're talking about in terms of styles and materials.

It all adds up to shopping smart, to collecting wisely, to getting more value and beauty for your decorating dollars. You'll get a higher return on the time and energy invested in making your house a home that, in turn, makes *you* look and feel terrific.

Rethinking Your Space, Room by Room

The whole of your home is greater than the sum of its many parts. It's refuge, rallying point, center of the social structure around which civilization has been built and over which wars have been fought.

Yet every home is made up of many parts, or rooms, each one serving a specific purpose, involving special kinds of furnishings, and a different approach to decorating. While the very names of the various rooms under our roofs give a clue to their use—*living* room, *dining* room, *bed*room, *bath* —even those basic functions are evolving and changing, along with so many other facets of 20th-century life.

Living Rooms—Rooms for Living

Of all the rooms in your home, the living room is the most public. It's where *you* will be seen most often as you receive visitors and entertain your guests, so set the stage for yourself with the colors that most flatter *you.*

Most living rooms fall into one of two categories: either they are mainly reserved for special, company occasions, or they are the rooms in which the family really *lives* every day. Also, in these times of shrinking floorspace, many living rooms have to double for dining or even for sleeping overnight guests.

How you will be using the space dictates not only its overall ambience— formal or informal—but also the specific kinds of furnishings you need, and how they will be arranged. To help you pin down just what it is that you want from your living room, consider these questions:

- Do you have to go through the living room to get to the other rooms in the house?

- Do you usually entertain guests in the living room (as opposed to family room, porch, or patio)?

- Are you a nut about keeping the living room in perfect order at all times in case someone drops in?

- Is this where you spend most of your leisure time at home?

Study your answers, and you'll have a pretty good idea of what kinds of furniture you'll want to use, and even what styles.

- Cul-de-sac living rooms are more easily set aside and kept company-ready than rooms through which everyday traffic must flow.

- If you like to entertain formally in the living room, choose furnishings that present the image you want to convey of your tastes and family life.

- If your own family spends most of its leisure time in the living room, then choose furnishings that are more easy-going and comfortable.

Overall ambience: Do your tastes, lifestyle, and season suggest that your living room should lean to the *formal* side, or toward the *less formal?* As a rule, Winters and Summers tend to the formal; Autumns and Springs, to the less formal.

What counts most in setting ambience is *attitude.* Do you admire furniture that demands respect? Are low-slung, slouchy furnishings your style? *Attitude* also stems from architecture. Rooms with symmetrical windows, a centrally located fireplace and French doors naturally feel more formal than ones with quirky architecture, or no interesting details at all. On the other hand, certain built-in features almost automatically set a casual mood: ceramic tile floors, open beams, and sliding glass doors, among them.

You really do have to acknowledge your room's architecture when you plan your furnishings, but you aren't locked into all contemporary just because you've bought space that is sleek and unadorned. The word for a compromise between architectural styles and furniture styles is *eclectic.* A word as old as the Greek from which it comes, eclectic means choosing the best from various sources. We've only recently begun to use it in talking about interior design, and what a great addition it is to our vocabularies.

Easily translated into living rooms, eclectic means a mix of contemporary and traditional styles. Since a living room is usually the largest in the house, it's really where you can best express your personal style.

You can start with contemporary upholstered pieces and blend in whatever traditional chairs and accessories suit your fancy and your season. Or, you can update an overall traditional theme with a contemporary piece, such as a glass or lacquered table.

Of course, if you live in an authentic 18th-century house or careful re-creation of one, by all means be a purist and use all the antiques or quality reproductions you can afford.

Thanks again to that magic word, *eclectic,* you don't have to go to either extreme. All the easy-going furnishings and fabrics available today will let you relax and be comfortable in the most formal living room. And the least formal can maintain its composure through thick, thin, and visiting children.

What colors? Once you know what kinds of furnishings you'll be using in your living room, and what mood you want to establish, study your palette again, looking for colors that will carry it out. Remember what we said earlier—

- Cool colors are somewhat more formal and reserved.
- Warm colors are more active and less formal.
- There are both warm and cool colors in every palette.

Entrance Halls—First Impressions

Whether it's a narrow hall or a grand entrance, indeed, this is the first glimpse anyone gets of your home—and of you—when you meet them at the door. To look great when you greet your guests, surround yourself with the colors that become you most, colors chosen straight from your palette and used liberally on walls and floor.

Of course, your entry should relate directly to the colors and furnishings in the living room just beyond, since chances are, both rooms will be seen at a single glance. *Here,* that glance will make an important impression, so be bold about using *your colors* and proclaiming *your style.*

One way to do that is with wallcovering that coordinates with the fabric in your living room. Such coordinates often come in a variety of styles and pattern sizes. You might use the smallest in the entry, since small patterns tend to stretch space. Or, go the other way and choose an over-scaled design. Really big patterns can play interesting tricks on very small spaces, giving them an air of importance far beyond their actual size.

Another way to tie your entrance hall into your living room decor is with color. Pick up the accent color you've used in *there*, and paint it on your walls in *here*. You will also want to choose a rug that's related in color and pattern to your living room. It doesn't have to match exactly, but it should give a hint of things to come.

There are two *practical* considerations about entry halls that are important to you and your guests:

1. *Convenience.* Provide somewhere to sit, if there's space—a bench, a chair, or even a small loveseat. Another welcome convenience would be a table, chest, or wall-hung shelf. If there's no closet nearby, a coat rack can be a good idea in more casual homes. A mirror is *always* a good idea, and lighting is essential, whether it comes from an overhead fixture or a lamp on the table or chest.

2. *Maintenance.* You'll love yourself for keeping your entry way as maintenance-easy as possible. Enough said.

Dining Rooms—Set for *You*

Never mind all the talk about the demise of the dining room—it's never been more central to our idea of *home*. Preoccupied as we are with good food and gracious living, the dining room has once again become a focal point in our family lives. And certainly, it's a rare woman who doesn't see herself as hostess, presiding over a candlelit table filled with glorious foods and surrounded by guests who are witty, charming, and admiring.

The cuisine and guest list are up to you, but we *can* tell you how to make yourself look admirable, indeed, in your dining room setting: color yourself beautiful with the best your palette has to offer.

Harmonizing spaces: If you'll be dining within view of the entry hall or living room—as often happens in center-hall colonials—or actually in an ell of the living room itself—you'll want to use colors that relate to the other spaces. They don't have to be totally repetitive, however, so you might want to repeat just one color or pattern. Or, use a coordinating pattern in the same color.

For example, a living room in *your* white and your favorite color would adapt beautifully to the dining room next door. In *there,* the walls would be white and the color in the fabric on a white background. Brought on in *here,* the color is in the wallcovering used above the chair rail. A coordinating fabric covers the chairs and the white of the living room walls is restated in the background of the rug.

Both rooms have their own distinct personalities, yet there are enough common denominators to give the separate spaces a pleasing harmony when the house is taken as a whole.

Separate tables: When your dining area is a room unto itself, with no color obligations to any other room, you can flex your imagination and bring in a fresh, new color scheme from your palette. Again, there are some general color truths to guide you:

- Dark colors will make dining a more intimate experience.
- White, light, and neutral colors are serene and soothing.
- Bright colors will create a more animated atmosphere.

A dining room is where you find it. Not every home is blessed with a separate room set aside just for dining, but don't despair. You can find room for gracious dining in a number of creative ways. It may be as simple as turning a corner of your living room into a dining area or keeping a drop-leaf table in your foyer. *Where* you dine matters less than *how.* Anywhere you surround yourself with *your colors,* you can look terrific and never mind that you may be serving on a desk that was doing home-office duties two hours earlier. We've even given dinner parties *in* our New York office conference room, made elegant with candlelight and flowers.

Dining in style: Mixing styles in a dining room can be very pleasing to the eye. Matched sets of furniture are an old idea anyway. Better to collect your dining furniture by individual pieces, as long as they have *attitude*—formal or informal—in common. A glass dining table mixes beautifully with French or English chairs. So does a Parsons table. Even your chairs don't have to match exactly, as long as they're fairly uniform in height and size (host and hostess chairs excepted).

Bring in serendipitous serving pieces, as well. A wall-hung shelf or narrow table could take over for the traditional sideboard. There are delightfully few hard-and-fast rules about what must go where in decorating today: dictums are out, imagination is in.

That goes for setting your table, too. Collect a wardrobe of table "linens" and an ensemble of different "props" for centerpieces so you can set an imaginative table to suit your mood and the occasion. Your "linens" can include table cloths, placemats, and napkins in *your colors*. No doubt, they won't really be *linen* in this blessed age of easy-care look-alikes, which means you get all the texture and feel of the real thing with less work. And your centerpiece can also be a far cry from the same old thing. We've seen everything from globes of swimming black mollies (sparkling on a glass table) to beautifully stark, bare branches, beribboned bunches of asparagus, and still lifes of turnips, gourds, and Indian corn . . . all imaginative and much more interesting than the old by-rote bowl of flowers.

Dining by the right light: To bring out the best in *your colors*—and you—add good lighting to your dining room menu. Chances are, it will be coming from a chandelier or hanging fixture over the table. Two caveats here:

1. Hang the fixture high enough so it won't glare in anyone's eyes while you're seated, low enough to relate to the dining area below. Between 34-36 inches above the table top should do it.

2. Use a dimmer switch to control the light level, so you can have efficient light when you're working around the table that dims to romantic levels while you dine.

More light on lighting will be shed on page 160. Meanwhile, back in the dining room, you should indulge in candles to supplement your other dining lights. Nothing makes a Winter more dramatic . . . a Summer softer . . . an Autumn more glowing . . . a Spring as radiant . . . than the flattering aura of flickering candlelight.

Bedrooms—The Intimate You

Bedrooms are not just for sleeping—at least not today. Once tucked off in the back of the house somewhere—remember the Victorians' sleeping porches?—bedrooms have gone back to being round-the-clock rooms. The French kings would approve: they often held court from under their royal covers, with petitioners lined up at bedside. And the earliest American pioneers would understand: their entire lives were lived in the bedroom, so to speak—it was essentially the only room in the house.

It still is, for some of us who live in efficiency apartments. But the rest of us retreat voluntarily to the bedroom, there to take off our public faces and relax into our private moments, alone or with a favorite partner.

Now that it's on 24-hour duty, the bedroom requires special attention to furniture and decor. The bed is just the centerpiece. Stereo equipment is apt to be in there, too, along with a TV, writing desk, or a seating area, complete with space for dining. There's even a demand for mini-refrigerators that masquerade as bedside stands so your midnight snack is always at your fingertips.

Since you'll be spending so much more time in here, by all means *color your bedroom you.* Pick up favorites from your palette and use them to create a background against which you'll look your loveliest around the clock.

Since this *is* your most personal, intimate room, more of your skin will be showing. Take plenty of time to try out various colors in your palette, living with large swatches of them before you make a color commitment. It's even worth your while to buy a small can of paint and color one wall so you can study it *in situ,* and appraise your reactions to it, both physically and emotionally. Here are two other points to remember:

- Calm colors create a serene mood, conducive to knitting-up emotionally, and to sleep. You can meld your light colors into a quiet scheme, or interplay your neutrals into a scheme that's both soporific and eloquent.

- Darker colors are inherently intimate and evocative of both faces of Night, its glamourous side and its sleepy side.

Some Suggestions to Sleep On

Aside from making *you* look terrific *en deshabille*, there are other criteria for the successfully dressed bedroom:

Furniture styles. Note the plural. Just as in your living and dining rooms, an eclectic mix of furniture is today's more interesting way to go.

The better bed. Whatever size you need, buy the best quality mattress and box springs you can afford. Period.

Roommaker beds. Because it is the centerpiece of the room, pay special attention to the style of your bed. Lucky you, if you're blessed with an antique, such as a canopy bed, a brass bed, or a sleigh bed. If you're not, be inventive. A new headboard will give both your bed and the entire room instant character. Some examples: white wicker or white wrought iron in a white-plus scheme; a *faux* canopy made of sheets and hung from a ceiling-mounted rod; a padded headboard slipcovered to match your comforter; any free-standing screen—spectacular for an island bed.

Bed-dressing. This is a wonderfully wide-open subject, with almost no end to the ensembles you can assemble for your bed. Wait till you have settled your background colors—walls and floor—before buying them, however; it's easier to find bedclothes that coordinate with them than vice versa. When you do shop for your bed, buy in multiples so you can mix and match almost at random. With all the coordinated collections available today, it's almost impossible to make a mistake. Some even offer wallcoverings and towels that work with your bed things. You can convey any mood you want, from strictly sleek and tailored to marvelously romantic and fey.

Peace and quiet. Important to the comfort quotient of any bedroom, sound and light-proofing measures focus on your walls and windows. Fabric-covered walls absorb sound; shirring the fabric is even more effective; quilting over thick padding and upholstering the walls are the ultimate answers to very bothersome noise problems. Carpeting can also help put the quietus on a bedroom, and if you live in an apartment, it's essential. Multiple layers of fabric also insulate windows against noise, light, and energy waste. Investigate all the new ideas in environmental window products before you settle on an old solution. You'll find aluminum-backed pleated blinds, insulated quilt panels that function like roller shades, and weather-blocking tinted film you apply to panes directly so you can even leave the windows bare if that's your look ... and if your outlook is worth it.

Bathrooms—Seeing Yourself At Your Best

Time was when the bathroom wasn't even allowed in the house! Today, it's become a hub of activity: we don't just bathe there anymore, we take a shower-massage or a whirlpool bath ... we go there to work out ... to mellow out ... even to indulge in a communal hot tub.

Today's bath is a personality room. Gone are the clinical white tile walls and antiseptic-looking fixtures. Color is in, in more ways than one. We can have it in exquisite ceramic tiles and bath "furniture" that looks more like sculptured accessories than the "necessaries" of life. Bath linens have gone high-style, as well. The same designer who does your clothes is writing his name across towels, shower curtains, and bath rugs. And count your blessings if you have old-fashioned fixtures. Pedestal sinks and footed tubs are eagerly sought collector's items, commanding respectable prices in antique stores. In fact, you can even find brand-new "oldies." Manufacturers have responded to our retro urge by bringing out reproduction models.

The point of all this: while it may be the smallest room in your house, your bath has a big decorative role to play. Here, you can afford to indulge your flights of fancy, so little material is required, decoratively speaking. Turn it into a spa, a sophisticated retreat, or a country corner. Anything your imagination can conjure, you can create with a few accessories and colors— *your colors.*

The bath is where you'll get the full benefit of *your colors* at work, standing nose-to-nose with your makeup mirror, completely immersed in the reflection of *your colors* from all four walls ... and ceiling. Don't forget the decorative value of the ceiling, especially here, where you want to create a feeling of intimacy anyway.

If you're planning a complete bathroom overhaul, try to find more space to throw into your new floor plan. It may be worth sacrificing an adjacent linen closet, or taking a bite out of a nearby bedroom. Realtors tell us that next to the kitchen, the bath is a major factor in evaluating your house, so you stand to recoup your investment should you sell.

Of course, most of us are concerned with redecorating, rather than re-doing. And there's a myriad of minor changes that can make a mighty big difference in the way your bath looks and functions. A checklist of idea starters includes:

- *Re-color your tiles.* You can do it with special epoxy paint in *your colors.* It takes time and patience, be warned, but the result will be well worth it.

- *Re-tile right over your old tiles.* There are new ceramic products that spare you the mess and money required to rip out the old and start again.

- *Replace your fixtures.* Marvelous new tubs, showers, sinks, and toilets can be installed by a plumber in short order.

- *Refresh your walls.* Vinyl or vinyl-coated wallcoverings are your best bet, since they stand up to the hothouse climate of a bath. Paint, wood, and plastic laminate panels can work wonders, too.

- *Renew your linen supply.* Lush, new towels in *your colors* can make a tepid bath look fresher and rejuvenated.

- *Recharge your lighting.* New fixtures, overhead and on *both* sides of the mirror, let you see things in a new light.

- *Reflect yourself.* Mirror tiles make great sense in any bath. Use adhesive if you put them up yourself: ordinary self-stick tabs won't keep their grip long in all this moisture.

- *Revamp your flooring.* Spread *your color* wall-to-wall with washable bath carpeting you can install yourself. Or, use resilient tiles, sheet flooring, or wood planks (if it works in a sauna, it can work in here).

- *Rethink your storage possibilities.* No bath seems to have enough. Study how you can put under-used space to work ... over the toilet tank, above the bathtub ... around the ceiling line ... under the sink. Your answer may be as simple as store-bought shelves and racks.

Kitchens—Cooking With Color

Like baths, kitchens haven't always been allowed under the same roof with the rest of our rooms. In colonial times, they were often banished across the backyard to a separate "cook house," primarily because everyone lived in fear of the fires that were left banked overnight on the hearth.

Kitchens have never been more *in* than today. They've become the heart of many homes, the first place everyone heads when we come into the house, and the last place we visit before we say goodnight. Credit our changing society for the change in the kitchen's status. The gourmet mania that's swept the nation has everyone back in the kitchen cooking up dishes that would make Brilliat-Savarin blush. But now that women are out of their aprons and into business suits, it's no surprise that, at the same time, we Americans are eating out more than ever. The paradox makes sense: cooking has become an *occasion*. The rest of the time, we go out.

The effect this has had on our kitchens is that they've become a social center, a gathering spot. You need more cooking *accoutrements* and more comfortable accommodations for kibitzers. Two-stove kitchens have the social status once reserved for two-car garages. And more dilettanti are trading up for professional equipment: huge restaurant stoves, matched sets of stainless steel and copper-bottomed cookware, plus the overhead butcher's racks to display them.

Simultaneous with this move toward high-tech efficiency in cooking gear, there's been a move back toward the friendly, comfortable kitchen of yesteryear. The country look doubtless heads the list of personality kitchens.

Evocative of the good old days, it grants poetic license to the romanticist: almost anything goes in a country kitchen, from a calico-covered couch by the woodburning stove, to rafters hung with dried herbs overhead. One good reason to love the country look: it thrives on clutter. So if you're shy of storage space anyway, and the look fits your season, this may be the theme for your kitchen.

There are other ways to go, as well. A kitchen can be the sleekest and most contemporary room in the house. New cabinet and counter materials (especially laminates) come in a rainbow of colors. The European look has influenced new cabinet styles that are clean and uncluttered, even down to non-existent knobs.

In between these two extremes — comfy country and clean-lined contemporary — there are endless ways to impose *your* personality on your kitchen and to color your background so that you look terrific even while slaving over a hot microwave oven.

There are three main kitchen areas to color: cabinets, floors, and countertops. In most kitchens, actual wallspace is miniscule, limited to soffits over the cabinets and an occasional break between appliances. The cabinets pretty much dictate your color scheme. If you can't live with them, now that you're aware of *your colors*, there are a number of ways to effect changes:

- *Paint.* Better than a brush or roller, a spray-painter makes a smooth job of re-coloring either wooden or metal cabinets so that they look brand-new.

- *Wallcovering.* Cover just the door fronts in a flattering plain texture or a print. Vinyl-coated coverings stand up best to kitchen life; otherwise, protect the surface with a couple of coats of polyurethane.

- *New cabinet doors.* For less than tearing everything out and starting all over, you can have new doors made for old cabinets. Colored or tinted glass could be interesting in either a traditional or contemporary kitchen. For a country atmosphere, consider punched tin—you can design it yourself with a hammer, nails, and paper pattern.

Floors for colorful kitchens can be made of almost any material that suits your mood. The only limiting factor nowadays is your tolerance for maintenance. Obviously, some flooring products demand less than others, one reason for resilients' perennial popularity. Another is the advent of cushioned floors that pamper your feet and aren't always fatal to dropped dishes. Resilients come both as tiles and roll-goods (we still say "linoleum," even though true linoleum is nearly extinct), and they're both available with a thousand faces. They can look like everything from quarry tile to slate, brick, and wide-planked pegged boards. Study all your options, and choose the one that carries forth the ambience you want to create.

Other good ideas for kitchen floors include the *naturals*—real brick, authentic slate, honest-to-goodness wood. If you've already got them, by all means, flaunt them. But if you're considering adding one of these natural floors, consider also the extra maintenance, noise, and wear-and-tear on the cook. Wood's the exception, thanks to the minor miracle of polyurethane varnishes that will render it impervious to the spills and splashes a kitchen floor is exposed to.

Ceramic tiles are also a natural for kitchen floors—and counter-tops—plus, they're easy on the maintenance crew. Like their resilient cousins, real ceramic tiles come in a gratifying variety of styles, sizes, and color choices.

A word about kitchen carpeting: the word is *gone*, at least, for wall-to-wall installations. They simply got grungy with time, despite all the claims to the contrary, because you couldn't pull them up for cleaning. Small scatter rugs, on the other hand, are a colorful addition to any kitchen floor. (And good for use under a table to set off the eat-in area.)

Redecorate or remodel? Up to now, we've concerned ourselves with kitchen facelifts, small projects you can accomplish yourself, rather than The Major Remodeling. Remodeling is not to be undertaken lightly. It's costly, time-consuming, and effectively puts this important room out of commission for days on end. However, if your back's against the wall—literally or emotionally—your time and money will be well spent on a remodeling job. Along with the bath, as we've mentioned, a great kitchen can really kick up the value of your entire home.

Family Rooms—Rooms for All

They've been around so long now, it's hard to realize that "family rooms" as such are really an American creation, made-up spaces that were added to our homes soon after World War II. It was a time when everyone was interested in togetherness, and wanted a room where grown-ups and children could relax together, while the more formal living room remained pristine and company-ready.

Parents Magazine gets credit for the name itself; before its editors coined the term "family room," such easy-living spaces were called "recreation rooms," "rumpus rooms," even "don't-say-no" rooms, according to a recent article in *The New York Times.* For our money, that hits it right on the head: every home needs a space where almost anything goes, a shirtsleeves kind of a room in which you can put up your feet and let down your hair, and parents don't have to say "No! don't . . . lie down on the sofa . . . bring that pizza in here . . . spread your puzzle all over," etc., etc., etc.

Homes built between the 1950s and the late 1970s almost automatically had an official family room included in the plans. At first it went down in the basement and later moved a step or two upstairs from the attached garage, or just off the kitchen. Today, with building costs soaring and space shrinking, the family room is often rolled into one so-called "Great Room" that may also include the living and dining rooms.

Wherever your family room is actually located, what matters is that you have an informal, at-home space somewhere under your roof, and that you fill it with equally relaxed furnishings. Even when there are no children to contend with, *you*'ll appreciate being able to live casually in here while the "living" room stays neat.

Planning your family room calls for another study of the people who will be using it, and how. Ask yourself the same questions you considered when you were laying out your living room:

- What will go on in there? TV? Meals? Music? Parties?
- What special furniture do you need?
- How much storage? For what? Books, records, games, video software, craft materials?
- Will the space be used mostly during the day or at night?
- Just how informal do you want the room to look?

Again, the answers to these questions will help you focus on how to go about choosing the right furnishings. Some helpful hints in that direction:

Living with video. Some experts suggest that television, not togetherness at all, gave rise to the family room. And certainly that's where most TV sets end up today, along with the video games, audio equipment, and the family computer. Decide whether or not the entertainment center is indeed going to be the center of attention in your family room, and if it is, make it the focal point around which you arrange the rest of the furniture. At least, include flexible seating pieces so you can shift your orientation from the TV to the fireplace or picture window, if you're blessed with either.

Carefree furnishings. Just because you want to create a *casual* atmosphere in your family room, don't think you must sacrifice all sense of *style*. Nearly everything comes worry-free today, from washable wallcoverings to velvets of manmade fibers, treated to shrug off the household misfortunes that family rooms are especially prone to. Shop smart in the first place, and this really can be a "don't-say-no" room. Look for:

- Soil-repellent-treated fabrics, carpets, and rugs.
- Tabletops finished so they shrug off water and alcohol.
- Furniture with tightly woven upholstery fabrics and slightly nubby surfaces for long wear (some of the manmades are especially good).
- Slipcovers you can zip off and on easily for washing or cleaning.

What about colors? Since the entire family is expected to use this room, you may have trouble being "selfish" enough to do it in your own palette, despite the good advice we gave you in the chapter "Color Considerations for Others You Live With." Neutrals are a good compromise, especially for a family room where there's apt to be a lot going on anyway. Look over the range of neutrals your entire family has in common, or nearly so, and mix in a lot of off-white (everybody's best white). If you still feel the need for more color, use one of the season-spanners for accent.

Making the Right Arrangements

When it comes to arranging your furnishings successfully in a room, to paraphrase an old lyric: "It's not what you have, it's the *way* that you have it."

The right room arrangement can make even stingy, broken-up spaces lovely to look at, delightful to live in. The wrong arrangement spoils both the room's beauty and its comfort. Happily, there are near-foolproof formulas to follow for the "right" room arrangement, no matter how limited or large your floor space. A *right* room arrangement is based on three main criteria:

1. Navigability
2. Convenience and comfort
3. Visual composition, or balance

Navigability

The flow of traffic in, out, and around the room depends on where the room is and how it's used. Stand in the doorway of the room you're about to arrange and list the answers to these questions:

- Is it a cul-de-sac, or will traffic need to move completely through the room and out another door?

- What allowances must be made for opening and closing windows, reaching closets, clearing radiators, air-conditioners, and hot-air ducts?

- Which way do the doors open (including closet doors)?

- How is this room going to be used, and by whom?

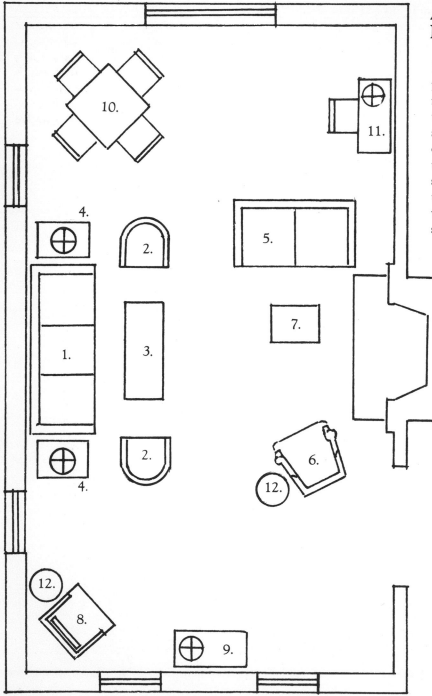

A Flexible Living Room Arrangement

In a traditional living room, the fireplace is the natural focal point of the room arrangement. Here, the sofa faces the fireplace, flanked by lamp tables and a pair of upholstered chairs, with a coffee table within easy reach, no matter where you're sitting. A secondary seating arrangement directly in front of the fireplace includes a love seat and wing chair, angled slightly toward the sofa.

A Flexible Living Room Arrangement

1. Sofa
2. Upholstered chair
3. Coffee table
4. End table
5. Love seat
6. Wing chair
7. Coffee table
8. Occasional chair
9. Console or chest
10. Game table/chairs
11. Secretary/chair
12. Side table

grouping to encourage conversation and add interest to the otherwise symmetrical arrangement. Note that each seating piece has a convenient table nearby, with adequate lighting from lamps well distributed around the room. This arrangement leaves space for a game table and chairs in one corner, a tall piece, such as a secretary and a chair that can be pulled into the conversation group when needed.

Within such a flexible arrangement, you can easily accommodate your special pieces of furniture. For example, if you have a piano, the love seat can move to where the wing chair is now, the wing chair could move to the corner where the game table is, and the opposite corner used for the piano.

Arranged for Comfortable Dining

Below: Since the dining table is the center of attention, place it to allow plenty of push-back room for the chairs all around. Storage and serving pieces should be within easy reach. Extra dining chairs can wait against the wall until they're needed for special occasions when the extra leaf is added to the table. A lovely touch when you have space is a wing chair in the corner, served by a low side table, and perhaps a plant on a decorative stand.

Arranged for Comfortable Dining

1. **Dining table**
2. **Side chair**
3. **Armchair**
4. **Sideboard or china**
5. **Server or buffet**
6. **Wing chair**
7. **Side table**
8. **Plant on stand**

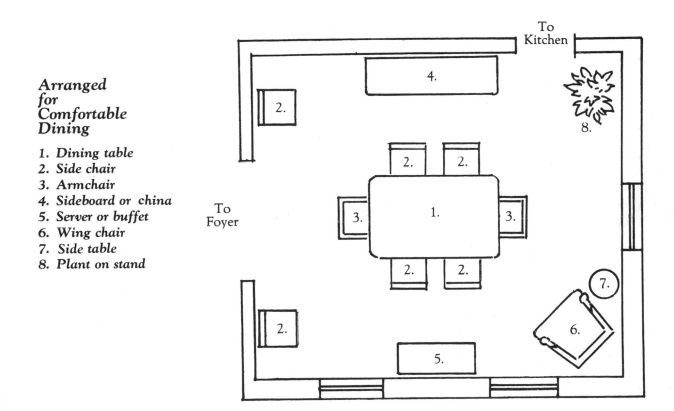

123

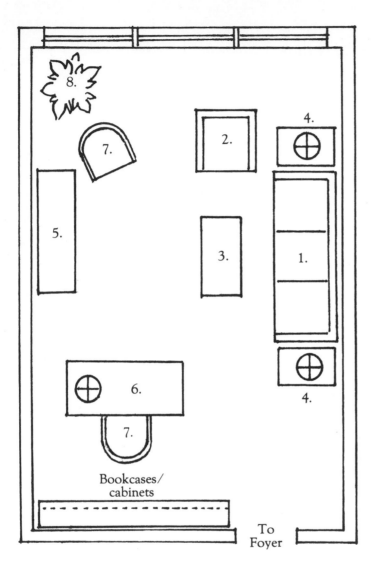

Bookcases/
cabinets

To
Foyer

A Living Room
with a Corner for Dining

The floorspace in an apartment may be limited, but not so living space, if you plan dual-purpose furniture and flexible arrangements. The sofa defines the living room; the writing table serves for both study and for dining, when the occasional chair is drawn up on the other side. The writing table can serve four when two chairs are brought in from another room. Bookcases behind the desk provide open storage. The cabinet on the other wall houses both bar and pull-out television.

A Living Room
with a
Corner for Dining

1. Sofa
2. Club chair
3. Coffee table
4. End table
5. Storage cabinet
6. Writing table
7. Pull-up chair
8. Plant

A Living Room with a Dining Area

Your best arrangement starts with the main seating area against the longest wall. In this L-shaped apartment living/dining room, the sofa is flanked by lamp tables and two upholstered chairs that can be swiveled to face the TV in the storage unit opposite. Because the dining area is narrow, a wall-hung shelf is used for serving in place of a sideboard or buffet.

A Living Room with a Dining Area

1. Sofa
2. Swivel chair
3. Coffee table
4. End tables
5. Storage cabinet
6. Dining table
7. Side chair
8. Wall-hung shelf
9. Plant

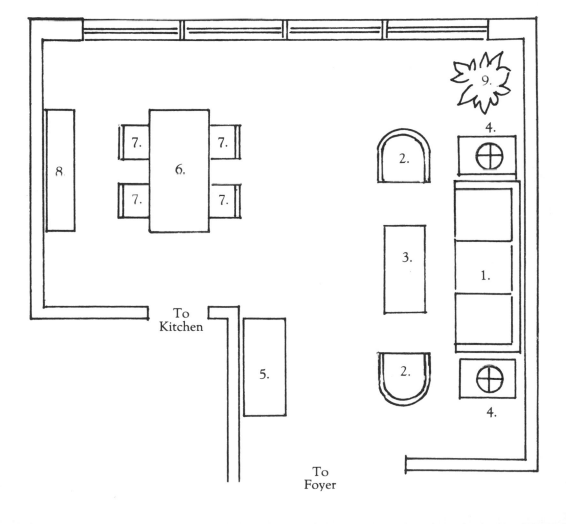

To Kitchen

To Foyer

Convenience and Comfort

Convenience and comfort are as directly related to how you arrange the furniture in a room as they are to your choice of furnishings in the first place. If you overcrowd the space so you have to squeeze in and around the furniture, you'll feel more claustrophobic than comfortable. Conversely, if the furniture's so sparse and spread out that you must commute from the sofa to the coffee table, or squint to read from a far-distant lamp, the inconvenience will become a major irritant.

To insure comfort and convenience, here's a checklist of the furniture you will need:

- *In a living room*, upholstered seating pieces are primary. You may choose a sofa and chairs, a sofa and love seat, two love seats, or an L-shaped sectional. It really depends on the space within which you're working. Once you've met your *comfort* needs, you will need the *convenience* pieces: end and side tables, coffee table, storage pieces, lamps. If your living room's really spacious, you may need a secondary seating area, or *activity* area. That could mean dining space, or a corner for a piano.

- *In a dining room*, the table and chairs are *de rigueur*, of course, along with a sideboard or buffet for storage and serving. If you have a large dining room, you may want to turn it into a dual-purpose room, introducing a small love seat and chairs.

- *In a bedroom*, you will need a bed, naturally, and a dresser or a chest, and perhaps a dressing table or a place to house the TV. If your bedroom is good-sized, a seating area is a lovely addition with a love seat and/or chairs, and table in the group.

Visual Composition

Visual composition, or balance, is the final—and very important—consideration in planning a room. Once you've analyzed what you want the space to do, who will be using it, and what pieces of furniture you need, you can set about setting those pieces into eye-pleasing arrangements that work as well as they look.

Planning Your Room's Composition

Plan first on paper and let your fingers do the pushing. Use graph paper where the scale is one-quarter inch to a foot of floor space, and furniture templates, also in the same scale.

Measure your room with a metal rule and mark it off on the graph paper. Be sure to note all permanent features: doors, windows, fireplace, built-ins, and electrical outlets.

Next, find a center of interest for your room arrangement. Your architecture is usually your clue. In a living room, a fireplace is a natural focal point, around which you can group your primary seating pieces. A window with a handsome view will do nicely, too. If your living room lacks natural attributes, you must *create* a center of interest. Works of art can be a good answer here. So can a special piece of furniture. Or, you can focus your seating group on *itself,* creating a self-contained conversational group that's obviously *the* place to be in the room.

In a dining room, the center of interest is usually the dining table, just as the bedroom naturally revolves around the bed itself.

Now, using your templates, begin laying out your room, keeping in mind that traffic lanes and doorway clearances should be at least 3 feet wide.

1. Settle your primary pieces.
2. Arrange your secondary pieces.
3. Add tables, lamps, and plants.

If you've already decided on your color scheme, crayon it onto your plan for overall balance, remembering that dark colors and woods carry more visual "weight" than light colors and woods. Remember also to distribute large- and small-scaled furniture throughout the room, rather than group like-size pieces together. Do allow for the vertical dimension: every plan needs some tall pieces, such as a highboy, armoire, etagere, or even a wall of art that pulls the eye up and down. Sometimes the very architecture of the room will provide the balance you need: a staircase, fireplace, or window could do the trick.

Here are some practical pointers and general measurements that will help in your arrangement-planning:

Living Room

- If your living room's more than 13 feet wide, you can place the sofa at right angles to the fireplace wall. When the space is narrower, put the sofa with its back against the longest wall.

- Chairs in a seating group should be no more than 8 feet apart for comfortable conversation, and should more or less face each other for good eye-contact.

- Each seating piece requires a table within easy reach, no more than 18 inches away.

- Side tables should be ½ to 2 inches below the arm of the sofa or chair.

- Allow at least 14 inches of knee-space between coffee table and the sofa or chairs.

- Heavy pieces (sofa or club chair) can sit half-on/half-off the edge of a rug.

- You'll need about 7 square feet of floor space around a game table to allow comfortable seating and push-back room.

Dining Room

- You'll need 3 feet of clear space around a dining room table for easy passage when the chairs are occupied.

- A rug used under the dining table should be 3 feet wider all around than the table so the chair legs don't slip off.

- Allow from 26 inches for side chairs; 30 inches for armchairs.

- A round table that seats two people should be 24 inches in diameter; for four, 36 inches; six, 48; for eight, 54.

Bedroom

- Allow 2-3 feet on either side of the bed (not counting night tables) for bed-making and getting in/out.

- In front of a dresser, you will need 40 inches; for opening a closet door, 36 inches.

Planning for Video Equipment

- The screen should be at, or slightly below, eye-level, except in a bedroom, where it can be somewhat above eye-level when you're lying down.

- Although the technology is improving, wide-screen TV is better watched from in front of the set, or slightly to the sides. Too steep a viewing angle may distort the picture.

- Stereo TV may require "outboard'" auxiliary speakers to achieve the stereo sound effect. Unlike audio speakers, which can be located anywhere, these must remain fairly close to the screen itself, or you'll be hearing the evening news over your shoulder!

Small Space Arrangements

Small-space room arrangements open a whole new bag of tricks. Try these and watch your space grow visually:

- Cover large pieces, such as sofas, to blend into the wall behind them.

- Search out double-duty furniture: coffee tables that rise to dining height; ottomans, chairs, and sofas that pop into beds; buffets with dining tables folded up inside.

- Opt for lighting that doesn't take up space on tables or floor: ceiling-hung fixtures, wall sconces, and the whole range of cove, cornice, and track lights.

- Put unused *high* spaces to work with overhead cabinets, extra-tall bookshelves, and display shelves around the ceiling line.

- Do a real make-over job on your closets, outfitting them with new fixtures and double-rods so every inch of space goes to work. In a bedroom, especially, maximizing closet space may allow you to get rid of a storage piece and free up floor space for a cozy seating group.

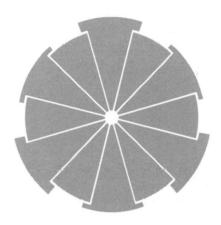

Designing a Victorian-flavored room for a teenaged Spring, Marianne Schmidt takes the color scheme from the wallcovering's floral design in ivory, coral pink, aqua, and periwinkle. The bed and windows are covered in ivory ruffles, and the slipper chair picks up the coral pink and periwinkle in its shadow check slipcover. The golden-blonde dresser and oil lamp are straight from Victoriana; the bedside table, from the designer's imagination: it's based on an antique sewing machine, painted coral pink. Another touch of the whimsy that's so right for this young Spring: the headboard is actually wood molding attached to the wall and painted coral pink.

CHAPTER VII

The Right Room Ingredients

Find *Your* Furniture

Books and books have been written on the history of furniture styles: where they came from, how they evolved, what distinguishes an early Chippendale, say, from a later masterpiece.

Don't expect to find that here. While furniture is the most fascinating of all the decorative arts (indeed, it comes closest to our own human form with its legs, arms, head, feet), discussing furniture styles in too much detail can be more confusing than helpful for the average home decorator.

You do need a working vocabulary of style names, and you should generally be able to recognize them at 20 paces on a showroom floor. But in these times of eclectic decorating, it's more important for you to recognize the prevailing *attitude* of a style of furniture, meaning, *is it formal or less formal?*

For one example of why these two broadbrush categories may be enough, let's look at the mahogany furniture of the Georgian Period, from the early 18th century through 1830 or so. An historian of the decorative arts would immediately begin dropping such names as Queen Anne, Chippendale, John Goddard of Newport, Rhode Island, or even Thomas Elfe, whose aristocratic pieces are still the pride of Charleston, South Carolina. To the historian, this magnificent period means cabriole legs, ball-and-claw feet, broken pediments and intricate fretwork. To an interior designer, however, the Georgian Period conjures visions of elegant *rooms*, rich with silks and satins, polished hardwood floors, and festooned windows. In a word: *formal.*

But wait a moment. This was also the time-span in which the American frontier was pushing west, when the colonists away from such sophisticated East Coast centers as Newport and Charleston were busily carving their own versions of Queen Anne and Chippendale, using native woods like maple, oak, and pine. These sometimes crude, now quite charming, pieces fit into the category broadly known as Early American. At least, that's the way our furniture historian would tell it. An interior designer, however, would think of Early American in terms of homespun fabrics, braided rugs, and strap curtains. In other words: *less formal.*

You see what we mean. You don't have to be an historian to furnish your home, but understanding where a certain look has come from—and why—is a large part of the fascination of interior design. It's simply more fun to know what you own or are buying.

Formal	Less Formal
The difference between **formal** *and* **less formal** *has to do with the details, materials, and craftsmanship. Look for fine grained woods, and more detail.*	*Less formal designs are apt to be executed in less refined woods and have less detail.*

Formal or Less Formal? A Guide to Furniture Attitudes

The difference between *formal* and *less formal* furniture styles lies more in the materials of which they are made and in the quality of craftsmanship, than in the basic design category.

Louis XV-style furniture is another example. When it was made for the court, the delicate, graceful pieces displayed regal breeding. They were made for only the best rooms in the land. But out in the provinces, the same style was interpreted in local woods by local craftsmen, and the result was a separate design category: French Provincial—or Country French—charming and elegant in its way, and above all, *less formal.*

There are also two ways of looking at most contemporary furniture. Take the same style of sofa or modular seating unit, upholster it in moire taffeta, and it's *formal.* Cover the same piece in linen, and it's *less formal.*

What's important here is the decorating flexibility this gives you within the general style categories that are best for your season. Such maneuverability allows for your individual tastes and needs without forcing you to stray from your optimal choices.

When you look over the furniture styles, remember what we said earlier: It's not what you have that determines the final effect—it's the *way* that you have it.

English Furniture

More Formal	Less Formal
William and Mary	Country English
Queen Anne	
Georgian, including:	
Chippendale	
Adam	
Hepplewhite	
Sheraton	
Regency	
Some Victorian	

American Furniture

More Formal

Colonial, including:
William & Mary
Queen Anne
Chippendale

Federal, including:
Hepplewhite
Sheraton

Directory

American Empire

Some Victorian

Some Modern

Some Contemporary

Less Formal

Early American

Mission

Shaker

American farmhouse

Some Victorian

Some Modern

Some Contemporary

French Furniture

More Formal

Louis XV

Louis XVI

Directoire

Empire

Less Formal

Provincial

or

Country

Other Styles

More Formal

Oriental

Biedermeier

Art Nouveau

Art Deco

Art Moderne

Less Formal

Scandinavian Modern

Spanish/Mexican

Wise buymanship:

- A piece of furniture must be at least 100 years old to qualify as a true "antique." Its value depends on how scarce and how well-preserved it is.

- Know the difference between *reproductions* and *adaptations:* the former is a line-for-line copy of an antique, while *adaptations* are indeed adapted to conform to present-day requirements of size, comfort, and construction. What's important here: reproductions may cost more, but then you may be buying the antique of the future.

- Always shop with your tape measure. Size up both your room at home and its doors—you'll be amazed at how often what people buy can't even get *into* the room.

- Don't believe that if a piece is veneered, it is of inferior quality. Veneering is an age-old technique that enhances the beauty of the piece since it allows for the use of exotic woodgrains and matching of grains.

- Read your hang tag carefully: product labeling, strictly enforced by the Federal Trade Commission, requires accurate information about the materials used. If a piece claims to be "all wood" or "all mahogany," it is. But if the tag says it's "mahogany-finished," it means only that whatever kind of wood was used is finished to look like mahogany.

- Solid wood is not a measure of quality. You may not even want it, except for legs and frameworks, since solid wood is subject to shrinking and swelling with the moisture in the air.

- "Simulated wood components" are not woods at all, but realistic look-alikes imprinted on vinyl, which is then firmly bonded to a core of either inexpensive wood, or non-wood. The finished piece is usually durable and inexpensive.

Buying quality in case pieces (all wood):

- Look at the back of the piece. It should be inset and screwed into the frame, or tacked with T-staples. Ordinary staples are a sign of inferior quality.

- All moving parts—table leaves, adjustable shelves, drop tops, drawers, and doors should operate smoothly, and be nicely finished all around.

- Drawer corners should be solidly joined with mortise-and-tenon, dovetailed, tongue-and-grooved, or double-doweled joins for longevity—not merely butted.

- Look under the piece. Are corners reinforced with screwed-and-glued-on blocks? Are there self-levelers on the legs?

- Finally, are grain patterns well matched? Is the finish deep, clear, and smooth? It requires up to 25 factory steps to get it that way, including hand-rubbing.

- Is the hardware tasteful, comfortable in your hand, and sturdy? On quality pieces, look for solid brass or pewter, and carved wood pulls.

Buying quality in upholstered furniture:

- Try the chair or sofa for size and comfort. Bounce, rock, stretch out. It should feel smooth all over (including the back and sides), and it should not squeak, moan, or otherwise complain.

- Study the fabric cover. Is the pattern well-matched all around? Do the cushions have zippers for better fit? Are weltings straight and securely sewn? Does the decking (beneath cushions) match the rest of the cover? Is the fabric tightly woven or sturdy enough for long wear? Is it surface-treated to repel soil and stains?

- Study the hang tag. Law also requires that filling materials be labeled. Of these, down is the most expensive, but while it's posh, it requires constant plumping. Good alternatives include cotton, polyurethane foam, and other manmade fiberfills.

- Ask about the inner construction: top quality pieces are made with either coil springs (8-way, hand-tied), or zigzag, or S-shaped, springs in the seat. The more here, the better. In the back, springs can be of lighter weight and somewhat different construction.

- Finally, look under the piece if you can and check for good frame construction, using the same criteria we just gave for case pieces. Frames should be solidly built of seasoned hardwood (ash, birch, elm, maple, and oak are good), not softwood, such as pine. There should be reinforcing corner blocks screwed and glued into place, and legs should be an integral part of the frame, not just attached to it. (If they are, you're dealing with second-rate quality.)

All About Walls

Walls do so much more for your rooms than just stand there holding up the ceiling. Decoratively speaking, they establish your color scheme and are big supporters of the overall mood in the room. Walls can be the easiest element to decorate in the first place, and the simplest to change when you want a fresh, new look.

What matters most is the color, texture, and pattern of your walls, not the kind of wallcovering you use. So *any season* can choose almost any material under discussion here, as long as you work within your palette and stay with your best textures.

Paint—Canned Magic

Paint is just the first of your wall options. For most home-decorating purposes, there are really just two types of paint:

- *Alkyd, or oil-based.* While the tradition persists that oil-based paints cover better and last longer, many paint experts recommend them primarily for old walls that may have many layers of "unknown origin" underneath. Oil paint, unlike water-based products, holds its own over anything.

- *Latex, or water-based.* Latex paints account for most of the home decorating market today, and with good reason: they're a delight to work with, odorless, quick-drying and easy to clean up with soap and water. You can paint the living room in the morning and hold a party there that night.

- *Epoxy* is a third kind of paint that could be of some interest to home decorators (see section on bathrooms), but epoxies are tricky to mix in the first place, and tedious to apply. Unless you count yourself an expert craftsperson, epoxies are best left in professional hands.

Whether you choose to deal in alkyd or latex paint, *finish* is an important consideration. There are five finishes, each especially well-suited to certain jobs:

1. *Flat, or matte.* When your walls are in near-perfect condition and you want a soft, dull finish.

2. *Eggshell.* A newcomer to the paint repertory that dries to a delicate, pebbly texture with low lustre.

3. *Low-lustre.* A soft, warm finish. Good for woodwork and trim.

4. *Semi-gloss.* Just what its name implies. Washable, so it's a natural for kitchen and bath walls, woodwork, and trim.

5. *High-gloss.* Most durable of all paint finishes, and highly decorative, with a hard, lacquer-like shine. Take care that your wall has a flawless complexion since the gloss accentuates every little blemish.

So much for the nitty-gritty of paint. Now that you know your medium, let's look at all the exciting ways you can use it.

Personal approaches to paint

While there are endless choices and combinations of colors in paint, there are two basic ways to use it in your rooms:

1. Paint the wall and trim to match. A good idea in small rooms or where you want a smooth, unbroken background that makes architectural irregularities disappear.

2. Paint the trim a color that contrasts with the wall so that the woodwork frames the room. The contrast can be slight—off-white trim for lilac walls for a Summer—or it can be sharp, as in white woodwork framing purple walls for a Winter.

Don't be shy about using one of *your colors* on the trim and applying *your* white to the walls themselves. This approach works best in traditional settings.

Combing

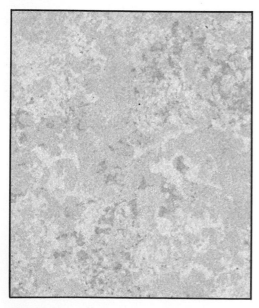

Sponging

Paint tricks

Paint is truly canned magic when you need special help with decorating problems. You can create separate areas in the same room simply by painting the walls (or just one wall) a different color. We've already told you how paint can lower or raise ceilings and push walls around, but you can also have fun with it—stretching your imagination to create special effects that personalize your living spaces and disguise less-than-perfect walls and floors. There are a number of techniques you can use, many of them as old as paint itself:

- *Combing or striating* a wall creates an interesting surface that can look as elegant as silk.

- *Sponging or stippling* is an earlier American wall treatment that's back in favor today.

- *Spatter painting and dribbling* are the answer for the "unartistic."

- *Stenciling* is another inexpensive way to add pattern to a wall or floor, or to furniture.

- *Texture paints* require absolutely *no talent.* They give a stucco-like finish straight from the can.

- *Marbelizing, faux bois, hand-painted murals* and *trompe l'oeil* are other special paint effects you should have in your vocabulary. These do require some skill, since their success depends upon their realism.

As we said so often, color is the most exciting, versatile decorating tool you can work with. Just think of paint as liquid color, and feel free to pour it on in fresh, new ways.

"Paint is not forever," smiles Ken Charbonneau of Benjamin Moore Paints. "It's still the least expensive way to change the entire mood of the room. If you make a mistake, you can afford to change it for the price of a few cans of paint. It's not like $1000 tied up in wall-to-wall carpeting—that's the kind of mistake a person would tend to live with!"

A colorful man in his own right, Charbonneau likes to tell the story of the red ceiling in his 19th-century Greenwich Village townhouse. "We painted nine different reds up there and lived with them . . . by day, by night, by the different seasons." The winner was a dark red, a handsome foil for the room's crystal chandelier, and for Charbonneau's actress wife, a Winter.

It was also an unwitting gift to the neighborhood. "We're on an upstairs floor," he laughs. "I often look out and see passersby pointing up at our red ceiling—it's the only thing they can see from down there."

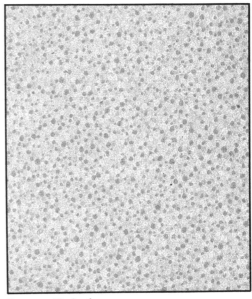

Spatter Painting

Stenciling

Wise buymanship:

- Study paint chips one at a time at home under the kind of day or artificial light it will be seen in. Remember that the color will look much more intense on a large area than on that tiny chip.

- Buy the smallest quantity you can and paint a two-foot-square test pattern on the wall.

- Once you've decided on the color, buy all the paint you think you need at the same time. Better to have some left for later repairs than to risk mixing colors in the middle of the job.

Wallcoverings—Rolled Magic

There's no other way to treat your walls to patterns and textures as beautifully—or as easily. Forget the old one-armed paperhanger routine! Today there are wallcoverings specifically designed for the hardly-handy-person to install easily with professional-looking results.

At the other end of the wallcovering spectrum are the elegant silks, textured "string" fabrics, and tactile grasscloths, ranging from smooth to nubby (which may require lining papers and special handling by a professional installer).

As you can see, it's not just wall*paper* anymore. In the parlance of the trade, wall*coverings* include all the flexible, decorative products you can use on a wall, whether they are paper, paper-backed fabrics, grasscloth, sliver-thin cork, or even wood.

There's so much new in *wallcoverings* today that you should treat yourself to a few hours investigating your options. Among the surprises in your dealer's sample books, you'll find coordinated wallcoverings, fabrics, and other decorative products that let you "do" entire rooms in one fell swoop: walls, windows, beds. With these preordained go-togethers, you simply can't make a mistake.

There's a practical side of wallcoverings to consider, too. So you'll be well-armed when you go shopping, here's a quick study:

- *Machine-printed.* Moderately priced and perfectly acceptable in the best-dressed rooms. The name means just what it says, as opposed to . . .

- *Hand-screened or hand-printed.* Usually more expensive, for obvious reasons. These wallcoverings are created on large versions of the traditional artists' silkscreen. You can feel the layers of paint on the surface.

- *Pre-pasted.* The adhesive is already on the back, so you simply dip the wallcovering in water to activate it, and hang. Many pre-pasted products are in the low-to-medium price range.

- *Wall squares.* New on today's market, wallcovering squares actually hark back to the very first type of wallpapers invented. Just a foot square and pre-pasted, they're easy for beginners to handle and make short work of small spaces.

- *Borders.* Also making a comeback, borders are ideal to finish off a wallcovering job, or can be used alone on a painted wall, around doors and windows, to make *faux* chair rails, or to liven up plain, painted furniture.

- *Pre-trimmed.* Whether wallcoverings are printed by machine or by hand, a slight selvage is required down each side for handling during the manufacturing process. Pre-trimmed products arrive with these borders cut off and ready for installation. Again, the majority of pre-trimmed wallcoverings are machine-printed; more expensive, hand-printed products usually leave the selvages on to protect the pattern during shipping and handling. It takes a steady hand, sharp razor, and metal straightedge to trim them—ask your wallcoverings dealer to do it for you.

- *Strippable.* Another revolutionary idea in wallcoverings are strippable (or peelable) products that can literally be peeled off the wall when you're ready for something new. However, unless it's especially heavy-duty vinyl, don't count on saving it for installation somewhere else. The advantage is in how easy it makes cleaning up old walls for something new.

- *Washable.* The arrival of vinyls to the art of wallcovering has brought with it new durability and "cleanability." Vinyl or vinyl-coated papers can stand up to repeated washings, if not outright *scrubbings.*

Personal approaches to wallcoverings

Here are some of the ways to work wonders with wallcoverings in your rooms:

- *Stretch space.* Vertically hung stripes push the ceiling up and make the room look taller and larger. Hang those same stripes horizontally around the room and watch those walls become longer. Openwork patterns such as trellises and window-pane checks also bring you to the optical conclusion that the room's more spacious than it really is. This trick is especially effective on a too-low ceiling.

- *Shrink space.* Dark-grounded busy designs and large, impressive patterns fill up the walls and lower the ceiling to make the room feel smaller and cozier. Border papers can be used to break up wall space and bring the room down to size. Apply borders on the wall around the ceiling line in place of architectural mouldings or apply them around the edge of the ceiling itself, a look the Victorians loved. Use a wide border to simulate a chair rail, especially effective in the dining room with two different, coordinating wallcoverings above and below.

- *Smooth out awful walls.* If your walls are anything but downright *crumbling*, chances are wallcovering will heal them. The right pattern and textured surface will hide multitudinous sins. If they are really rough, install lining paper first, or look for new cushion-backed wallcoverings that can even be hung smoothly over rough concrete or cinder block walls. One warning: when you're dealing with a rugged surface, avoid foils and other metallic wallcoverings, and any with a shiny, light-catching finish. They'll highlight everything ugly underneath. If your walls are bad and you want to save your patterns for furniture and floor, consider a strie or ombre wallcovering with a definite texture.

- *Go off the wall.* You can cover your kitchen cabinets, unfinished furniture (Parsons tables are a great bet here), and we've even seen floors wearing wallcoverings under a protective coat of clear polyurethane. Save your wallcovering scraps for small decorative accessories—picture mats, waste baskets, and desk accessories.

Wise buymanship:

- Measure very carefully, including all nooks and crannies to be covered. Use a metal rule and measure the distance in feet all around the room. Measure the height of walls. Make a rough sketch of the room, including all windows, doors and openings, such as a fireplace or bookshelves. Note your measurements on the sketch, and take it with you when you order the wallcovering; your dealer can give you an exact number of rolls to order.

- Wallcoverings usually come in double-roll bolts. Each roll covers approximately 30 square feet, allowing for trimming and pattern match. With a large repeat in the pattern, you will get less coverage, so figure accordingly.

- Subtract one-half roll for every window and door in the room.

- If in doubt, *over*-order. Subsequent reorders will cost time, and the dye lots may vary. Besides, most dealers will let you return unopened bolts. Ask in advance.

- Vinyl and vinyl-coated wallcoverings are your best idea for high-traffic areas, even though some of today's vinyls could pass for delicate silks and damasks.

Other Ways with Walls

When most people say "wallcoverings," they're talking about the flexible kind that comes in rolls. Don't stop there. Depending on your season, your room, and the mood you want to create, you should investigate rigid coverings, too.

- *Paneling.* Today's paneling falls into two categories: real wood (expensive but beautiful) and manmade lookalikes that are actually quite durable, easier to install yourself, and certainly less expensive. They're a good answer to badly blemished walls and action-prone areas, such as children's and family rooms. Don't be put off if you think the finish looks too *faux:* a coat of paint will give the illusion that there's real wood underneath.

- *Mirrors.* Wall-sized mirror panels are expensive and usually require professional installation, but are a good way to stretch space visually.

- *Fabric.* Walls upholstered or covered with fabric are warm, posh, and quiet, since the material serves to help deaden sounds. Whether you start with yard goods, or sheets, there are three best ways to apply fabric to your walls: *glue it up,* using vinyl paste; *staple it up* in panels that are either flat against the wall or gathered; *hang it on rods* by sewing a narrow channel at the top and bottom of the panels.

The Lowdown on Floors

Floors are your room's fifth wall, much too important to be stepped over lightly when it comes to carrying out a decorative scheme. A sleek, gleaming wood floor sets a very different pace than plush wall-to-wall carpeting ... quarry tiles evoke another mood ... a rich Oriental rug yet another. As you have seen, some of these moods and textures work better for *your* season than others, making them almost as important as selecting *your colors* in floor-coverings.

A quick overview of what's what in floors today is in order:

Soft Floorcoverings

Soft floorcoverings fall into two categories:

- *Carpets.* Usually room-size or wall-to-wall, available in a variety of surface textures, designs and fibers (wool, synthetic fibers, or a blend).

- *Rugs.* Smaller in actual size, but varying enormously in style and type. For example, machine-made and handwoven Orientals and the so-called ethnic types—dhurries, kilims, Berbers and American Indian, mainly the Navajos. The ethnic rugs are usually made of natural fibers—wool and cotton—while machine-made rugs of modern manufacture are likely to be wool, synthetic fibers, or a blend.

Within these two broad categories of soft floorcoverings, you can enjoy a wealth of choices in colors, patterns, textures, and prices. There's something here for every season.

Your choice between wall-to-wall carpeting and a smaller rug can be guided by the size of the room itself. Allover carpeting is a good way to stretch space visually in small rooms, and to tie spaces together in an unbroken sweep of color (for instance, between the living and dining rooms in a smaller home). Room-size rugs are enjoying great favor today because it's interesting to see a bit of the floor all around the rug. They're also practical for a society that's constantly on the move. If you choose a room-size rug, calculate to leave a foot or so of bare space on either side, and a bit more, about 16 inches, on the ends. An area rug can be any size, as long as it's in proportion to the furniture you use with it. In a living room seating area, for example, the rug should define the area around a sofa, chairs, and coffee table.

An attractive alternative to buying a rug off the rack is to order one custom-made and colored to echo other designs in your room. A less expensive option is to order a solid rug with a border in another color. It's possible to change that border color later, should you want an entirely different look without spending a lot of money.

While we're on the subject of budgets, a word about the cost of floor-coverings. They will represent a good share of your total budget anyway, so buy the best quality you can possibly afford. It will repay you in service and beauty over the long run. Of course, you should expect to pay dearly for a rare, old Oriental as you're buying a work of handmade art, but there are perfectly acceptable and affordable machine-made Oriental-*style* rugs manu-factured in the U.S. Comparatively low price tags are one reason for the current popularity of ethnic rugs — you can buy a lot of style for the money. As a general guide to pricing carpets by the yard, wool leads the way in cost. Cotton, which used to be the least expensive, is gaining in both chic and price. The manmade fibers (acrylic, modacrylic, nylon, polyester, and olefin) tend to be more moderately priced, though price and quality vary considerably.

Whatever the fiber, it's the *way* it has been treated that accounts for the finished appearance of the carpet or rug. There are a confusing number of different pile treatments for tufted carpets alone. Suffice it to say that whatever kind of carpet or rug you are considering:

- Plush, smooth finishes look formal.
- Textured and flat finishes are less formal.

Hard Floorcoverings

Hard floorcoverings include the naturals—wood, ceramic tiles, slate, marble, and brick—and the resilients, which are manmade. As with soft floorcoverings, it's the *finish* that makes ceramic tile and resilient floors look more or less formal. Highly glazed, solid colors are definitely formal and sophisticated. Picture, for instance, a Winter's foyer in stark black-and-white squares with a crystalline shine, compared to the medium-lustre, unglazed quarry tiles that are better for an Autumn. There are literally hundreds of styles, shapes, sizes, and colors to choose from in both authentic ceramic tile or its manmade cousin, resilient tile.

Resilients also come in sheet goods (what we still call linoleum), even though today's version is made of either vinyl or vinyl asbestos (v/a). Solid vinyl is more expensive because the color goes all the way through. On less-costly v/a products, it's the thickness of the vinyl surface that determines both the wear and the price tag. While resilient floors still have a long way to go, they do have two very endearing features: they are cushioned for underfoot comfort, and treated with finishes that refuse to be waxed.

Real ceramic tiles are coming up in the world of floorcoverings, after years in the kitchen and bath. They appear in the dressier areas of the home, thanks in large part to California and Sun Belt tastemakers. Picture a sunny dining room or glassed-over sun porch floored in Summer's off-white ceramic tiles, or in Spring's ivory.

Wood, perhaps our first love in flooring, belongs to every season, though the color and finish should fit your palette. New wood flooring can now be installed over old, provided it's reasonably smooth and level. You can choose strip flooring in random narrow widths, wide planks up to 12 inches, or parquet squares, some of which even have foam backing that makes them easy on both feet *and* ears.

While there are certain styles of floorcoverings that may work best for your season, your final choice will depend on whether you want a more or less formal look.

Among the more formal floorcoverings are:

- Velvet carpeting
- Oriental rugs
- Patterned rugs
- Sculptured rugs
- Solid-color velvet rugs with border design

Your less formal choices include:

- Textured carpeting
- Sisal matting
- Ethnic rugs
- Braided rugs
- Rag rugs
- Painted floorcloths

Wise buymanship:

- You will hear the words "denier" and "ply" when discussing carpets. *Denier* refers to the size and weight of the fiber. *Ply* is the number of fiber strands that have been twisted together to form a single yarn. As a rule, the higher the numbers for denier and ply, the better the quality of the carpet.

- The thicker and denser the pile, the better it will wear.

- Test it by bending back a corner: the backing shouldn't "grin" at you.

- The label on the carpet or rug is often your best source of information. It should tell where the product was made and exactly what fibers were used. With blends, the majority fiber will be given first.

- Most authentic Oriental rugs are made of wool, often woven on a cotton warp.

- The more knots per square inch, the better the Oriental.

- The pile of a good Oriental should be silky and smooth, and the rug itself supple and easy to fold.

- The fringe on an authentic Oriental is an integral part of the rug, not sewn on later.

- Always use high-quality padding or cushion under any carpet or rug. It may be made of animal hair felt (expensive and allergy-provoking), of fiber felt (least expensive and least durable), or of foam-rubber or sponge-rubber (both soft underfoot and long-wearing). Newest of the cushioning materials is a pad made of small, gas-filled polyester fibers bonded together.

- Most new carpets and rugs come with guarantees from both the manufacturer of the fiber used and of the product itself. Get your guarantee in writing and file it with your sales slip.

- Many new carpets also come with special protective treatments to help repel soil, stains, and moths. If the one you love does not, inquire about having it treated before it moves in with you.

Windows for All Seasons

Of all the architectural features with which your rooms are blessed (or cursed), windows are the most important. They can also be the most demanding. Whether they're lovely enough to provide the focal point for your entire room arrangement, or so homely you'd like to hide them, windows are vital ingredients in your decorative scheme.

Window Treatments

The first step toward your best window treatment is to study the anatomy of the windows themselves. Are they the classic six-over-nine colonial double-hung, narrow clerestories, floor-to-ceiling cathedral windows, bays, bows, arches, or mere holes in the wall? If yours are unique, be glad. This adds character to your room without unreasonable problems, thanks in large part to the proliferation of window hardware and new freedom in decorative styles. There's a rod for every type of window, and a curtain, blind, or shade, ready-made and waiting to be hung. And, if you have them made, your options are virtually unlimited.

Your choices should be guided by three practical considerations:

1. *The view.* Is it worth showing off? If so, you want treatments that frame, rather than obscure. Will the inside view be more interesting than what lies beyond the window? In this case, you can cover a good portion of the glass. Where a window is very small and unimpressive, extend your dressing onto the wall itself to make it look bigger.

2. *Light, air, and privacy.* Will you be using the room in the daytime enough to depend on the light from its windows? Are you hermetically sealed for air conditioning and heat, or do you need ventilation? How much privacy-control do you need?

   Your answers here will tell you whether you should opt for flexible window treatments that can be adjusted to meet your needs, or whether you should consider more rigid, fixed coverings. Examples: shojii screens, folding shutters, or (neighbors and weather permitting) no window covering at all!

3. *Decorative statement.* What is the overall mood you are trying to express in the rest of the room? Your windows have a big say in carrying forth that theme. For example, swags and jabots *say* formal elegance . . . tieback curtains under a shaped cornice *are* 18th-century colonial . . . lace curtains *bespeak* old-fashioned romance. Your choice of window treatments must be in keeping with your basic decorative statement and at the same time suit the window style itself.

When it comes to choosing window treatments that will carry forth a formal or less formal mood in your room, select your fabric carefully. It has more to do with the degree of formality than the actual *style* of the window dressing itself.

Among the best looks for more formal rooms are:

- Curtains: straight panels or tie-backs, used alone or with:

    Cornices

    Festoons

    Swags and jabots

- Lambrequins, upholstered or painted
- Fabric shades, Roman or balloon

No matter what your season, any of these window treatments will work in less formal rooms:

- Curtains: straight panels or tie-backs, used alone or with a simple valance
- Blinds (vertical, mini-slats, matchstick, woven wood)

- Louvered shutters, painted or stained
- Shades (accordian, soft-pleated, and roller)
- Screens (sliding and folding)

Wise buymanship:

- If you decide to buy your curtains or draperies, instead of sewing them yourself, you have several options:

  1. Store-bought ready-mades, which are least expensive, but usually fit only standard-size windows.

  2. Special-order, or made-to-measure, which are made up in your choice of fabric to fit your measurements.

  3. Workroom custom-mades, which cost about twice as much as ready-mades, but offer unlimited choices of fabrics, styles, and sizes. Plus, the workroom (a retail store or decorator shop) can send someone to your house to take measurements, and install the window treatment when it's finished.

- If you're buying ready-mades or made-to-measure curtains or draperies, measure your windows individually—they can vary, even in the same room. And do use a non-stretching steel tape. It's also a good idea to take a sketch of your window along with you when you shop.

- There are three correct lengths for curtains: to the windowsill, to the bottom of the apron on the window frame, and to the floor. A fourth option is to let curtains spill a few inches onto the floor, European-style, but this look is appropriate only for more formal rooms.

- For all but the sheerest treatments, linings are worth the extra cost. They conserve energy, make the curtain panels hang more smoothly, protect the fabric itself from the sun, and look more attractive from the outside.

- Choose fabrics carefully. Look for fiber content on labels, and be sure to file all information on maintenance and care. Finishes are important, too: they can add body, repel moths, inhibit mildew, and prevent wrinkles.

- Checkpoints for quality in curtains or draperies include: straight hems, square corners, stitching that is neat and straight, and patterns that match, both on individual panels and from one panel to the other when they are hung.

- There are three basic types of rods: stationary curtain rods, traverse rods that draw, and decorative poles. Always buy the best window hardware you can afford—it will pay for itself in the long run.

- Window shades are available in both translucent and opaque weights. Your choice depends on the amount of light-control you need.

- You can also order shades with the roller reversed, so they present a smooth face to the room.

- Blinds fall into three basic categories: woven woods, venetians, and verticals. Woven woods feature long strips of natural or painted wood held together with decorative yarns in a choice of colors. Venetian blinds also come in a range of materials and styles, from mini-slats in a rainbow of colors, to fabric-laminates, filigrees, and real wood slats. Vertical blinds may be made of translucent or opaque shade cloth, fabric-laminates, and painted or shiny metals.

The Very Fabric of Your Rooms

Fabrics are many decorative elements rolled into one. They provide the colors, textures, and patterns that give your room its visual interest. It's the fabrics, in large part, that account for the pervading personality of the room.

Which fabrics you choose to interpret your season's colors depends on your answers to questions like:

- Do you want a more or a less formal ambience?

- Are your basic furnishings traditional, contemporary, or an eclectic mix of both?

- What kind of wear and tear will the fabricked areas undergo?

In general, it's pleasing to see a variety of fabrics used for slipcovers, at the windows, on chair seats, and such. A variety of surface textures is more visually interesting, but when you work out your fabric mix, be sure to keep them all in the same basic *mood*. They should be formal or less formal, depending on whether your room is traditional, contemporary, or a blend of both. As always in decorating, there can be occasional exceptions to even that rule: a float of sheer lace at the window will take the hard edge off the most contemporary room, for example. And a contemporary tone-on-tone linen can bring a classic French armchair fast-forward into today's lifestyle.

Fabrics that look and feel *more* on the formal side include:

- Brocade
- Brocatelle
- Damask
- Velvet
- Moire
- Taffeta

Into the *less* formal category fall such fabrics as:

- Polished cotton
- Plain cottons or blends
- Textures (twills, slubs, linens)
- Corduroy
- Wool flannel
- Leathers (suedes and Ultrasuedes)

Wise buymanship:

- Heavier materials with denser weaves and/or thicker surface piles (such as velvet) should be used for upholstery.
- Slipcover fabrics should be durable but not stiff, especially if you favor shirring or a gathered skirt.
- Sheer fabrics will filter natural light at the window; if you use heavy materials, accept the fact that you'll be darkening the room.
- Be sure to allow for pattern matching when you order fabric for furniture or curtains. A very large pattern repeat can mean a lot of wasted fabric.
- Protective surface finishes that repel stains and soiling will make any fabric much nicer to live with for a longer time.

Enlightenments

Lighting is perhaps the most often used—yet the most under-utilized decorative element of all.

It exerts tremendous influence over the way your room looks and feels . . . warm and cheerful, exciting and dramatic, or dreary and uncomfortable. Lighting also plays tricks with *your colors*, which is why we've been cautioning you all along to study your fabric and paint samples at home, in the light where they'll be seen.

Consider the source, literally, when you study your lighting. As a general rule, incandescent bulbs give off a warm yellow or ivory light. Fluorescents came into the lighting world emanating a ghoulish, cold-white light, but are now available in several shades, including "deluxe warm white," which is quite flattering to most complexions.

Good lighting at home comes down to three major types:

1. *Ambient,* or "walking-around" lighting, usually supplied by ceiling fixtures, including cove, cornice and valance lights, and lamps.

2. *Task lighting,* which comes most often from table and floor lamps focused on a specific area, such as a reading chair or desk.

3. *Accent* lights are small, hidden fixtures that give added texture, depth, and drama to your rooms. They may be recessed into the ceiling (downlights), put on the floor (uplights), or mounted on the wall or ceiling (spotlights).

Style and proportion are your major considerations when it comes to buying ambient or task lighting. In a traditional room, or one where you've set a definite theme, such as country, you'll want lighting fixtures and lamps that blend gracefully into the scene. But don't work overtime to find something with a lot of personality. It's better, far better, to err on the *conservative side* when you're choosing light sources. There are a lot of dreadful lighting fixtures on the market that can be very seductive when you're shopping. Your best shapes are still the basics and you can never go wrong with any of these:

- Candlestick
- Ginger jar
- Urn
- Column
- Canister

You'll find these five lamp silhouettes interpreted in many materials and colors, topped with shades that vary from gathered fabrics to pleated parchment.

Hanging Fixtures

Hanging fixtures and chandeliers can be a challenge. Your best guide here is the mood of the room. Is it formal or less formal? Crystal, polished brass, Venetian glass and that ilk are ideal for more formal scenes. Wood, wrought iron, stained glass, etc., should "hang out" in less formal rooms. Pay attention to proportion here. Hanging fixtures should be neither too large or too small for their space.

The best shapes for lamps

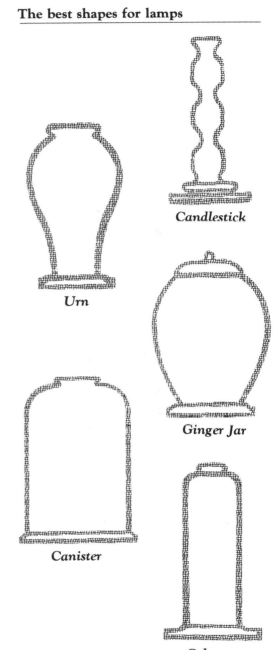

Candlestick

Urn

Ginger Jar

Canister

Column

Floor Lamps

Floor lamps and sconces can meet special needs. Both are good where space is shy. Two old-fashioned kinds of floor lamps are currently in the spotlight themselves: torcheres, which throw light up over the ceiling, and pharmacy lamps with goose necks that bend to light specific areas.

While they are not exactly sconces, track lights (mounted on wall or ceiling) provide lighting for specific tasks. They can highlight a painting or illuminate an activity area, or they can simply contribute to the ambient lighting level. Important points about track lighting: it is now available with light "cans" in a variety of styles and can work equally well in traditional or contemporary or eclectic rooms.

Wise buymanship:

- Buy lamps in proportion to the table on which they will sit. *Take your table measurements with you when you shop.*

- A lamp should never be as high as the table is tall.

- A lamp should never be so short you can look down on the bulb when you're standing.

- Hanging fixtures, especially over a dining table, should be high enough so they won't glare in your eyes when you're seated, but low enough to relate to the table grouping.

- *Always* add a dimmer switch to dining room fixtures.

- Remember that dark colors absorb light; provide more light if your walls and ceiling are dark.

- Opaque lamp shades throw light sharply up and down, while translucent shades provide general illumination for a larger area.

- Bedside lamps should be short enough to keep you from squinting up at the bulbs when you're lying down.

Accessories—Your Personal Finishing Touch

Your accessories bring your individual taste and personality into focus. Choosing your accessories is not just "decorating," but putting your own signature on the place. What you choose to show off in your rooms should be what *you* cherish and enjoy—*your* collectibles, *your* mementos, the works of art and the objects that speak to *you*, and of *you*. The only true rule governing what you live with is: if you love it, have it.

However, we offer two guidelines on how to display whatever you collect most effectively in your home:

1. Organize your collections and set aside a special spot for display (tabletop, bookshelf, or mantel).

2. Vary sizes and shapes within groupings, but plan a common color denominator or unifying theme that pulls them together.

The whole idea behind accessories is to catch and hold the eye and the imagination. Minimalists may insist otherwise, but it's these small, personal touches that give a room its depth, its texture, its very personality.

The Art of Hanging Art

Works of art are among the most personal accessories you add to a room. Not only do they give it a finished, lived-in look, but they also tell *who* lives here and what you cherish enough to have on constant display. However, *what* you hang is no more important than *how* you do it. Treated right, even inexpensive reproductions and posters can be as attractive as true master works.

Here are a few hints on how to group and hang your works of art artfully:

• Art is most effective when it adds a vertical thrust to the room, that is, when the individual pieces are taller than they are wide, or when a grouping of several pieces follows a vertical line.

- A single painting or framed piece should usually be hung at eye-level, about 5½ feet from the floor. When you're hanging something over a table or credenza, allow 8 to 12 inches between the bottom of the frame and the top of the furniture.

- Try to avoid hanging two pictures together if they're exactly the same size. Far more interesting: introduce a third, differently sized piece between the two. Three pieces of like size are fine, but hang them side-by-side.

- If you only have two equally proportioned pictures, hang one above the other.

- If you have two pictures of different sizes, put the larger one on top.

- Avoid "stair-stepping" pictures up a wall; this works only on a stair wall itself.

- To hang a grouping, plan first on paper. Tape brown wrapping paper together until it's the size of the wall space you want to cover. Working on the floor, lay your artworks out on the paper until you're pleased with the arrangement. Then trace around the frames, and mark the exact spot where the nail will go on the hanging wire once the picture is hung. Finally, tape the paper on the wall, and drive the nails right through the paper.

- A final hint: mark your target with an X of masking tape before you drive a nail. It will keep paint and plaster from crumbling.

Hanging Pictures

Vertical pictures give the room "a lift."

So will vertical arrangements of pictures. When two pictures are of different sizes, hang the larger one on top.

Two pictures of identical size look better one above the other than side-by-side.

Three pictures of identical size can be hung side-by-side.

Photo courtesy SCHUMACHER

Bedrooms aren't just for sleeping anymore. By making the utmost of your closet space, you may be able to trade a storage piece in for an intimate seating area like this. Quietly elegant with French overtones, it's a perfect Summer's retreat for quiet little candlelit dinners, or just relaxing with a good book away from the more public parts of the house.

CHAPTER VII

Do You Need an Interior Designer?

You may have a good idea of the look you want to live with—and by now should certainly know which colors and furniture styles become you most. But do you still feel you want help in pulling them all together? A professional interior designer can do that for you. Facing major structural changes or bewildering space problems? A designer can give you professional advice here, too.

You may simply need someone to hold your hand, someone whose taste and judgment you trust. A designer is that someone, and more. Psychological counseling, it's agreed, is a major part of a designer's job. We have designer friends who dine out on the tales of marital spats over fabric . . . of a husband who beat his head on the wall till his wife agreed on red carpet . . . and of children who want their rooms painted black, windows and all.

You can be assured, however, that designers won't tell names, as well as tales. They're professionals, after all, and respect their clients' private lives, however unusual they may be, decoratively speaking. This brings up another point: a good designer will be able to factor in all these personal preferences, and still come up with a room that *works*.

A designer may actually save you money by saving you from mistakes. He or she will know beforehand that the sofa you think you want will be too big for the freight elevator, let alone, your living room. And that the "antique" you're willing to break your budget for is really just a good reproduction.

Besides, a designer knows what's currently available, and where, and usually has a crew of reliable workmen and workrooms to handle whatever custom work your decorating projects will require.

A designer can certainly save wear and tear on your nerves, because he or she can take over the entire job, hiring and supervising painters and carpenters, ordering custom-made furniture, and making sure everything is delivered at the same time, so your room's not in constant upheaval.

If you're worried about how much this will cost, don't be. There are a number of ways to work with an interior designer that won't cost you any more than it would if you went out and bought everything yourself. Department stores and large furniture operations often have designers on staff whose expertise you can tap, free of charge. You may be expected to pay a retainer fee up front, but this is usually refunded after you have spent a certain amount in the store. The one disadvantage of working with an in-store designer is that you are expected to buy nearly everything from that particular store.

Independent designers work in a number of different ways and their fees vary according to their reputation, experience, and method of operation. Don't be shy about discussing all of this in great detail before you actually get involved. And don't hesitate to be explicit about how much money you plan to spend on the total job.

If your budget is really tight, you might want to pay a designer a flat fee (which could range anywhere from about $25 to $65 an hour and up) to come into your home and give you ideas on how to rearrange furniture, on window treatments, and color coordination. You buy those ideas with that fee, and take over from there.

Another option is to work out a purchasing agreement with your designer. This means that the designer buys everything—furniture, fabric, wallcovering—at wholesale prices; you pay retail or less. The difference becomes the designer's profit. Still other designers may work for a percentage of the total cost of your project, including labor and all purchases.

A designer will often work out a simple floor plan at no extra charge. However, if you want a detailed drawing or "rendering" of the way the finished room will look, be prepared to pay extra.

Also, be prepared to give the designer a deposit (up to 50 percent is usual) on any custom merchandise you order. And don't expect to get your money back if you change your mind. Chances are the designer has already made arrangements for the manufacturer to begin processing your order.

Finding a Designer

Finding a designer is not unlike finding a doctor or lawyer: it's important for you to trust and like that person. Call the local chapter of the American Society of Interior Designers (ASID) for their referral list. Ask friends for recommendations, pick up designers' cards as you tour local showhouses, and study the model rooms in department and furniture stores. When you see one you'd like to live in, a room that has an overall atmosphere that appeals to you and seems realistic for your home and family, call the designer and ask for a date. It should be the beginning of a love affair. But if it's not, once you've met and talked things over, keep looking. Remember, this person will be privy to your fantasies, family affairs, and financial state, so be as selective as you would be when choosing a new friend.

A new bath can be a terrific investment, in both your own comfort now, and in the market value of your house later. Tiled floor-to-ceiling in soothing colors, this master-bath addition features a deep, round whirlpool tub and a glorious greenhouse window that repeats its graceful curves. A harvest of colorful pillows, tiny garden of live plants and artworks on the walls make this a bath for all seasons to relax and recycle the spirits in.

The Best Is Yet To Come . . .

Now, you are ready to take on one of the most rewarding projects in the world: creating a very personal home environment that will bring out the very best in you.

We mean that in more ways than one.

When you *look* beautiful—as you will surrounded by your perfect colors—you will *feel* beautiful. Environment, as we have long known, is a powerful influence. It affects our attitudes toward life, in general, and ourselves, in particular.

Color *yours* beautiful, and you color *you* beautiful, inside and out.

GLOSSARY
Home Decorating Terms

A

Accessories   The small elements in a room that add individuality.

Acrylic   A manmade chemical fiber found under various trade names.

Adam   The brothers Adam, Robert and James, were late 18th-century English architects who came home from studies in Italy to lead the return to classicism in houses and furnishings.

Adaptation   Inspired by an antique.

Advancing Colors   Warm colors—red, yellow, and orange — that make surfaces appear closer or larger. Dark colors have a similar effect.

Analagous   Colors that lie near each other on the color wheel.

Antique   Officially, according to U.S. Customs Law, anything more than 100 years old.

Antiqued   Furniture painted or stained and distressed to achieve the worn, mellow look that comes with age.

Area Rug   Small rug which, as its name implies, is used to set off a special area.

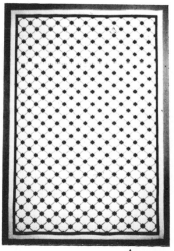

Area rug

Armoire

Bachelor's chest

Bail

Armoire (arm-*wahr*) Tall cabinet with two doors. Originated in France for the storage of tools and now used for everything from clothes to TV.

Art Deco (ar-*deh*-ko) Design form from the Twenties, revitalized in the Seventies, the Art Deco movement sought to use the design motifs of the industrial machine age in a decorative manner.

Art Nouveau (ar-noo-*vo*) "New Art," literally, when it emerged around 1900 with sensuous, swirling lines borrowed from plant tendrils. Enjoyed a renaissance in the late 1960s.

ASID American Society of Interior Designers. Professional organization for interior designers headquartered at 1430 Broadway, New York, N.Y. 10018

B

Bachelor's Chest A small chest of drawers.

Bail Curved metal handle, often attached to a backplate.

Ball-and-Claw (or claw-and-ball) Chinese motif of a dragon's claw clutching a pearl used by the English and changed to an eagle's claw by 18th-century American designers.

Ball-and-Claw

Bamboo A treelike tropical grass with woody, jointed, and often hollow stems used in making furniture.

Banquette A long upholstered seat built along a wall, usually for dining.

Barcelona Chair Now-classic leather chair on X-shaped steel supports, designed by architect Mies Van der Rohe and first shown in Barcelona, Spain in 1929.

Barcelona chair

Bauhaus (bough-house) Famous German school of design founded in 1919 by Walter Gropius. It is still influential today though it was closed by World War II.

Bentwood As the name implies, wood bent and shaped under steam and pressure. Process developed in the 19th century and put to good use by Michael Thonet, an Austrian furniture designer who is best known for his chairs.

Bentwood chairs

Berber A rug of undyed off-white wool yarn, flat woven, usually in a horizontal ribbed effect.

Bergere (bear-jhair) Wide, wood-framed upholstered armchair. The French word actually means shepherdess, whose wide skirts such chairs were made to accommodate.

Biedermeier (bee-der-mi-er) Neoclassic style of furniture from 19th-century Austria, named after a philistine comic character in a Viennese newspaper.

Bergere

Block Front Desks, chests, secretaries, with fronts made of thick boards that are cut in a series of three curves—convex, concave, convex. Most often found on American pieces and attributed to cabinetmaker John Goddard of Newport, Rhode Island.

Bow back chair

Bracket foot

Broken pediment

Bombe (bom-*bay*) French, meaning "blown-out," and usually applied to chests which bulge out in front.

Bow Back Chair Chair with back shaped like an archer's bow, usually with arms formed by another "bow" extending around the back.

Bracket Foot Simple, square foot formed by two pieces of wood angled together at the corner.

Braided Rugs These rugs date back to the American colonies and beyond into old Europe. In an effort to recycle cloth, strips of material were joined together. The strips were plaited and bound together, usually into an oval or a circle.

Breakfront Large, tall storage unit with lower cabinet topped by shelves enclosed by glass.

Breuer, Marcel Working first at the famed Bauhaus school in pre-WW II Germany, Breuer created metal furniture still admired for its simplicity and function.

Broadloom Carpet woven on a broad loom. Today's ads might indicate otherwise, but it is *not* a standard of quality.

Brocade Elegant fabric with woven, all-over raised design of figures or flowers.

Brocatelle (brock-a-*tel*) Flat fabric woven with two different yarns to create a puffed effect on the surface.

Broken Pediment A triangular pediment interrupted at the peak, sometimes filled with a decorative element.

C

Camelback

Camelback An upholstered chair or sofa with top curved like a camel's hump.

Cabriole Leg (cab-ree-*ole*) Gracefully curving leg with rounded knee, which takes its name from a French dancing term. Used by 18th-century furniture makers in England and America.

Cabriole leg

Cane Flexible rattan, woven for chair seats, backs, and cabinet doors.

Canopy Bed A tester, or tall four-poster bed with fabric canopy, sometimes with side curtains.

Cesca Chair Tubular steel chair with cane seat and back, designed by Marcel Breuer in 1928 and named for his daughter.

Chaise-Longue French word for an elongated lounging chair.

China Buffet topped with shelves to display china, sometimes enclosed with glass.

Chinoiserie (shin-*wahz*-o-ree) Decoration in the Chinese manner, particularly as done by admirers of China in 18th-century England and Italy.

Chintz Glazed cotton fabric often with flower designs. The name comes from the Hindu word for "spotted."

Chippendale, Thomas A London cabinet-maker who published a book of English furniture designs in 1754 that turned his name into a famous style.

Club Chair A comfortable, well-upholstered easy chair.

Coffee Table A low table used in front of a sofa for the service of coffee and other beverages.

Colonial American furnishings from 1700 to 1781. Also known as American Georgian, it is the era personified by Colonial Williamsburg.

Comb Back Chair Chair with top rail shaped like a comb, usually with a braced back.

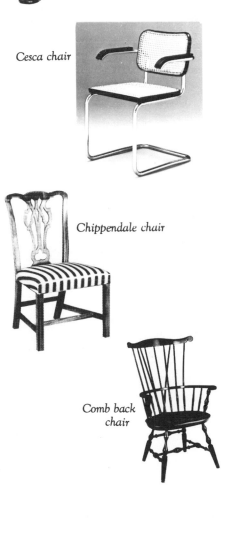

Cesca chair

Chippendale chair

Comb back chair

Console

Cornice

Combing A decorative finish achieved with paint to produce a striped effect.

Complementary Colors Colors that lie directly opposite each other on the color wheel.

Console A table used against a wall, sometimes supported by legs or brackets in front only. Can be used in an entrance hall or as a serving piece in a dining room.

Contemporary Furnishings designed and made today, of today's materials. Often a synonym for Modern, although Modern generally means the kind of form-follows-function design that began with the Bauhaus.

Country A nostalgic attitude that began in the 1970's to sweep the country, paralleling the overall back-to-basics movement. Typical country rooms include quilts, rag rugs, folk art, but country can also have a more sophisticated side.

Cool Colors Blue, green, and violet or any color to which blue has been added.

Cornice A wood frame, padded and upholstered, used to conceal curtain headings.

Crewel Twisted yarn used for embroidery.

Cube Neat little boxes in a variety of materials, used as small tables, sculpture supports, etc.

Cupboard *See China.*

D

Dado (*day*-do) When lower part of a wall is decorated differently from top, it is called a dado.

Damask   Firm, glossy fabric with flat design. It has been used ever since Marco Polo opened the fabric trade between Damascus and the Western World.

Dhurrie Rugs   Flat, reversible rugs with geometric motifs in soft colors, usually woven in India by hand. The new dhurries are made of wool. A dhurrie that is 50 years old is considered an antique and will always be made of cotton.

Directoire   (deer-reck-*twar*)   Period following the French Revolution (1792-1804), characterized by simple classic furniture that made the transition from the Neoclassicism of Louis XVI to Napoleon's Empire style.

Director's Chair   Wood or metal armchair with canvas sling seat and back that folds flat, scissors-style. Hollywood made it a star.

Directory   Period when the French Directoire influenced American furniture makers, producing a master of the style in Duncan Phyfe.

Distressed   Furniture scarred and painted to look old.

Drop Handle   Pendant handle, usually of metal. Also called tear drop.

Drop Leaf   Table with hinged leaves that can be raised to extend top area.

E

Eames, Charles   20th-century designer best known for his now-classic contour lounge chair of moulded plywood and leather.

Directoire tray stand

Drop leaf table (Queen Anne)

Drop handle

Eames chair

Your
Colors
At
Home
179

Empire chair

Etagere

Fauteuil

Finial

Early American   The furniture of the first settlers in the New World (1608-1720) which was a provincial version of 17th-century English styles; made in maple, oak, or pine.

Eclectic   (ek-*lek*-tik)   A mixture of furnishings from different periods and places carefully chosen to produce an interesting blend.

Empire   Napoleon's style. American Empire also revived Classic motifs from ancient Greece and Rome, and threw in some Egyptian flavor for good measure.

Escutcheon   (es-*kutch*-un)   Protective metal keyhole cover.

Etagere   (ay-ta-*jehr*)   French word for open shelves, either freestanding or hanging.

F

Faience   (fay-*ahnz*)   Tin-glazed earthenware. The term comes from Faenza, Italy, but was adopted for ceramics made in France.

Faille   (file)   Fabric with a crosswise rib effect.

Fauteuil   (fo-*too*-ee)   French word for armchair. Upholstered, but with open arms, as opposed to the bergere.

Faux Bois   (foh-*bwha*)   A decorative finish imitative of wood, achieved with paint.

Federal   Elegant, classic furniture that flourished in America after the Revolution (about 1781-1830). Influenced by England (Hepplewhite and Sheraton) and France (Directoire and Empire).

Finial   A decorative finishing element usually used on bedposts.

Flame Stitch Undulating, multi-colored pattern adapted from a traditional Hungarian needlework stitch.

Focal Point Anything of visual interest, such as a fireplace.

Foyer An entrance hall.

Fretwork Lattice work, usually in geometric designs; a motif borrowed from the Chinese.

G

Gateleg Table Drop-leaf table with legs that swing, gate-like, to support the leaves.

Georgian Period during the reign of all four Georges of England (1715-1830) when Chippendale, Sheraton, the Adam Brothers and Hepplewhite were making design history.

Glaze A transparent top coat of paint used to modify a base coat.

Gray, Eileen A pioneer of contemporary furniture design who produced her own tubular steel furniture in her Paris studio as early as 1922.

H

Hepplewhite, George A London cabinet maker who worked in the mid-to-late 18th century and produced dignified and refined furniture.

Flame stitch

Eileen Gray tables

Hepplewhite chair

Highboy
(Queen Anne)

Highboy   Tall chest of drawers, mounted on a long-legged commode or lowboy.

Hitchcock Chair   Painted and stenciled chair originally made by Lambert Hitchcock of Connecticut, who produced them in the early 19th century.

Hue   Synonym for color—red is a hue.

I

Intensity   The strength of a color. The difference between pink and red is a matter of intensity.

J

Jabot   (jha-*bow*)   Folded fabric cut diagonally across the bottom and used at sides of swag window treatment.

Jacquard   (*jack*-kard)   Intricate method of weaving invented in early 19th century by J. J. M. Jacquard and still used for such fabrics as brocade, brocatelle, and damask.

Hitchcock chairs

Jabot

K

Kas   Large cupboards, Dutch or Pennsylvania Dutch, with paintings or carvings.

Kilim Rugs   Flat, reversible rugs with geometric or floral motifs in bold colors, woven by hand of fine quality wool. Kilims differ from dhurries in that their weave is much finer and allows for more intricate designs.

Knocked Down (K.D.)   Furniture sent unassembled from the factory to be put together by the store or purchaser.

L

Lacquer An Oriental technique of varnishing furniture to a brilliant finish, borrowed and popularized by the English and French in the 18th century and very popular today.

Ladder-back Chair back with a series of ladder-like horizontal supports.

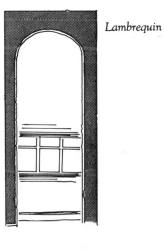

Ladder back chairs

Lambrequin (*lam*-bree-kin) Decorative frame for a window, usually made of wood, painted or covered in fabric or wallpaper.

Laminate Two or more materials bonded together under heat and pressure.

Lingerie Chest See Semanier

Lambrequin

Louis XIV—or Louis Quatorze (kat-torce) The "Sun King" of France (1643-1715) who built Versailles palace and filled it with grandiose, gilded, baroque furnishings.

Louis XV—Or Louis Quinze (kanz) King of France (1715-1774) whose reign is synonymous with rococo and its delicate curvilinear styles as seen in this handsome armchair.

Louis XVI—or Louis Seize (sez) Ruled France from 1774-1793 and during his reign brought back straight lines and classic motifs.

Love Seat A small sofa, not longer than 66 inches.

Louis XV chair

Louis XVI chair

*Lowboy
(Queen Anne)*

Matelasse

Occassional table

Lowboy   Low chest of drawers on long legs.

Lucite®   Trade name for clear acrylic plastic.

M

Marbling   A decorative finish imitative of marble, achieved with paint.

Matelasse   (mat-la-*say*)   Fabric woven so that it has a quilted surface effect.

Matte   A flat paint finish with no shine or luster.

Mission   Simple dark oak furniture named for Spanish missions in early California.

Modern   An approach to furnishings (art, architecture) which lets the function of an object dictate its form, eliminating any unnecessary frills and emphasizing the material used. Modern embraces all objects so designed, while "contemporary" is more of the moment, what is happening now. The terms are often used interchangeably, even by the experts.

Modular   Furniture with various components in standard sizes so they can easily be combined to suit individual needs.

Moire   (mwa-*ray*)   Fabric with a watermarked appearance.

Monochromatic   All of one color, or various shades of one color.

N

Navajo Rugs   These American Indian rugs have similar characteristics to the dhurrie. Once woven only in natural colors of wool, they can now be found in a greater variety of colors. The designs are mostly basic geometrics.

Needlepoint Embroidery with wool on heavy fabric. It may be done with fine stitches (petit point), or larger stitches (gros point).

Neoclassic Literally "new" classic: thus, classic forms revived, as during the French Empire period.

Neutral Colors The uncolors—whites, beiges, grays, browns.

O

Objet d'Art (ob-jay-*dar*) Adopted French term for any small art objects.

Occasional Furniture Small pieces that are only used occasionally.

Ogee Foot Shaped like a bracket foot, but with a double curve.

Ombre (om-*bray*) Striped fabric, using one color in several shades.

Oriental Rugs Rugs handmade in the Middle and Far East. Generally divided into six major groups: Persian, Bokhara, Turkish, Caucasian, Chinese, and Indian. Within each group are rugs named for the district or town where they were made; i.e. Kashan, Kirman, and Saruk are among the better-known Persian rugs.

Ottoman Armless and backless low seating, usually completely upholstered.

P

Paisley Multi-colored, comma-shaped motif borrowed from the town of Paisley, Scotland, where it first adorned shawls.

Parquet Wood flooring laid in decorative designs.

Ogee foot

Ottoman

Paisley

Parsons table

Duncan Phyfe chair

Queen Anne chair

Parsons Table Simple, squared-off table developed by and named for the Parsons School of Interior Design. Also known as a T-square table.

Patina (*pat*-e-na) Soft, mellow finish on furniture and metal caused by age and use.

Pedestal A center support for a table top.

Phyfe, Duncan One of America's first "name" designers. He was born in Scotland but worked in New York City from 1790 until 1847.

Plexiglas® Registered trademark for clear acrylic material.

Post Modern Literally, "after modern," meaning a return to many of the classic, established forms and furnishings we were living with before the form-follows-function dictates of the 20th century. Empire and Biedermeier furniture, marble, and columns are a part of the Post Modern look.

Primary Colors The three colors—red, yellow, and blue—from which all others are derived.

Provincial Copies made in the provinces of furnishings popular in the more sophisticated cities.

Pull-up Chair Occasional armchair to be pulled into use as needed.

Q

Queen Anne Queen of England for just 12 years (1702-14), she's immortalized in design history by the graceful furniture she favored.

R

Rag Rugs   These rugs date beyond the American colonies. To recycle cloth, strips of material were joined together to become the weft that was then woven through cotton or linen wrap threads. Very popular today.

Rattan   A climbing palm with long, slender tough stems which are used in making furniture.

Recamier   (reh-cah-myeh)   Chaise-longue with one end higher than the other. Named after Madame Recamier who reclines upon such a chaise in her famous portrait.

Receding Colors   Cool colors—blue, green, and violet — that make surfaces appear further away or smaller. Light colors have a similar effect.

Regency   England's version (1780-1820) of the neoclassicism that was sweeping the design world, later producing the Empire period in France and the Federal period in America.

Related Colors   Colors that are monochromatic or analogous.

Reproduction   A faithful copy of an antique.

Roman Shade   Window treatment with straight, tailored folds.

Rya Rugs   Shag rugs handwoven in the Scandinavian countries blend a deep pile and a flat weave. Once woven only in natural wool colors, they are now available in a wider range.

S

Saarinen, Eero   Finnish-born architect who is equally well-known for his spare, highly functional furniture designs, like this pedestal chair.

Regency chair

Saarinen chair

Saarinen tables

Your Colors At Home

*Country French
Secretary*

Semanier

Saarinen Table Sculptured plastic pedestal table designed by Eero Saarinen in 1960.

Sateen Cotton fabric with a glossy surface and dull back, often used for slipcovers.

Scandinavian Modern Simple furniture devoid of ornamentation and made of oiled woods— usually teak.

Scotchgard® Trade name for an oil and water repellent fabric finish.

Secondary Colors Colors created by mixing equal parts of two primary colors—orange, green, violet.

Secretary Desk with drop front writing surface, drawers below and shelves above.

Settee A small sofa, not longer than 66 inches, on legs with an exposed wood frame.

Semanier (sa-man-*yeh*) Tall narrow chest with seven drawers, one for each day of the week, as the French word for week, *semain*, implies.

Shade Any color to which black has been added.

Shaker Simply designed furniture made by the Shakers, a religious sect in America during the 18th- and 19th centuries. Very much to contemporary taste, copies are produced today.

*Shaker
rocker*

Sheraton, Thomas The last of the furniture designers who made England famous during the Georgian Period. Sheraton (1751-1806) has been called the "high priest of the straight line." He also published a book that spread his fame and style.

Shield Back Chair back shaped like an open shield.

Sideboard Originally a board, literally, for the serving of food; now usually has drawers or doors beneath for storage.

Sisal Straw-like fiber from a tropical plant used for matting.

Sleigh Bed 19th-century American bed with rolled headboard and footboard similar to sleigh front.

Slipper Chair Low, armless upholstered chair supposedly designed for putting on one's shoes.

Spatter-Painting A decorative finish in which colors are spattered over a solid ground.

Splat The major vertical support in a chair back.

Sheraton Chairs showing carving to look like bamboo

Hepplewhite Sideboard

Sleigh bed

Slipper chairs

Stretcher

Sponging   A decorative finish achieved with paint, giving a lightly flecked appearance.

Sofa   An upholstered couch with a fixed back and arms. A standard sofa is about 84 inches.

Sofa Table   Long, narrow table sometimes with drawers or drop-leaf, used in back of a sofa.

Stenciling   A decorative technique in which a surface is covered with a stencil design.

Stretcher   Wood or metal strip connecting furniture legs.

Strie   (stri-ay)   Fabric with random stripes, slightly different in color from the background.

Swag   Draped fabric used at a window, often with side jabots.

Swatch   Sample cutting of fabric.

T

Taffeta   A fine plain-weave fabric smooth on both sides, usually with a sheen on its surface.

Tallboy   A tall chest of drawers sometimes constructed in two sections.

Teflon®   Tradename for a moisture and stain-resistant finish.

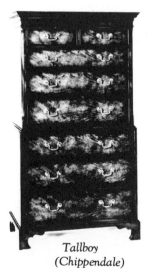

Tallboy
(Chippendale)

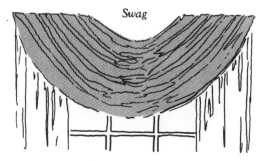

Swag

Tertiary Colors created by mixing equal parts of a secondary color with a primary color—red-orange, yellow-orange, yellow-green, blue-green, blue-violet, and red-violet.

Tint Any color to which white has been added.

Tole Tin or other metal, decorated and painted in various colors.

Torchere (tor-*shair*) Floor lamp that throws all its light upward.

Traditional Style of decorating inspired by the past.

Transitional Style of decorating showing the transition from one style to another and containing elements of both.

Trestle Table Long table supported by uprights at each end, attached to a heavy horizontal stretcher.

Trompe L'Oeil (tromp-*loy*) A decorative illusion "to fool the eye."

Tub Chair A chair with a rounded back.

U

Ultrasuede® Trade name for a man-made suede fabric.

V

Valance Shirred fabric used to conceal curtain headings.

Value The lightness or darkness of a color.

Van der Rohe, Mies A 20th-century architect who designed clean-lined modern furniture, such as the Barcelona chair.

Torchere

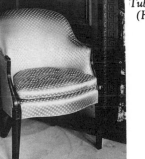

*Tub chair
(Hepplewhite)*

Valance

Wegner chair

William and Mary chest

Wing chair

Velvet   Fabric with thick, short surface pile, plain back.

Veneer   A method of furniture construction. A thin layer of fine wood or other decorative material is applied over a foundation material.

Victorian   The period from 1837 to 1901 when Queen Victoria ruled England. The era is marked by extravagant eclecticism, more accurately called hodge-podge. Furnishings were as stiff and formal as the manners of the day, but not always without a kind of charm that makes them enjoyable today.

W

Warm Colors   Red, yellow, and orange or any color to which yellow has been added.

Wainscot   (*wains*-sket)   Wooden paneling for interior walls, especially paneling that only reaches part-way up the walls.

Wegner, Hans   A Danish designer whose beautifully carved chair (1949) fired American enthusiasm for Scandinavian Modern furniture.

Wicker   Any thin, flexible twig woven together to make baskets and furniture.

William and Mary   Period (ca. 1689-1702) when English furniture began to grow lighter and less ornate, as French influence replaced the Dutch baroque.

Windsor Chair   Windsor, England, supposedly gave birth to this all-wood chair, but it won its fame in America where the colonists turned out many varieties, such as the bow back and the comb back.

Wing Chair   An upholstered chair with high back and projecting sides originally designed to keep out the draft. Still a popular style today.

RESOURCES

Finding a Color Consultant

The following color/image companies can direct you to a trained professional analyst in your area:

BEAUTY FOR ALL SEASONS, P.O. Box 309, Idaho Falls, ID 83402

COLOR ME A SEASON, INC., 1070A Shary Circle, Concord, CA 94518

COLOR ME BEAUTIFUL, INC., 5812 Tennyson Drive, McLean, VA 22101

FASHION ACADEMY, 1640 Adams Avenue, Costa Mesa, CA 92626

Finding Decorative Products in *Your* Season's Colors:

To make it easy for you to find what you need to decorate in *your colors* and *your style*, we are putting together a home furnishings collection keyed to your season.

For information, send a stamped, self-addressed envelope to:

YOUR COLORS AT HOME, c/o Acropolis Books Ltd 2400 17th Street, N.W. Washington, D.C. 20009

Finding *Your* Furniture Styles

Whatever style of furniture suits your season best, you'll have no trouble finding it for your home, thanks to the versatility of today's furniture industry. We are especially grateful to the following manufacturers, whose products illustrate the range of furniture styles shown in this book.

Baker Furniture Co.
Council Craftsmen, Inc.
Drexel Heritage Furnishings, Inc.
DSI International
Ethan Allen Inc.
Grange Furniture, Inc.
Guy Chaddock & Co.
Henkel-Harris Co.
Henredon Furniture Industries, Inc.
Herman Miller, Inc.
H. C. Gulden Mfg. Co.
Hickory Chair Co.
Hitchcock Chair Co.
Kindel Furniture Company
Kittinger Company
Knoll International
Nichols & Stone
Stendig, Inc.
Smith & Watson
Southwood Reproductions
Suter's of Virginia
Thomasville Furniture Industries, Inc.
Wood & Hogan
Wright Table Company

Your Colors At Home Products

Exclusive *Your Colors At Home* products are available from the following manufacturers at department and speciality stores nationwide.

Bath Ensembles:
    Shower Curtains, Sink Skirts,
    Bathroom Curtains, & Coordinates

        Ex-Cell Home Fashions, Inc.
        261 Fifth Avenue
        New York, NY 10016

        By Appointment
        261 Fifth Avenue
        New York, NY 10016

Bed Ensembles:
    Comforters, Bed Skirts, Pillow
    Shams, Table Rounds, & Curtains

        Pillowtex Corporation
        4111 Mint Way
        Dallas, TX 75237

Decorative Pillows:
    Pillows & Chair Pads

        Linde
        261 Fifth Avenue
        New York, NY 10016

Vases:

        Ceramic Fashions, Inc.
        230 Fifth Avenue
        New York, NY 10001

Your Colors At Home is a reg. TM of Lauren Smith, Inc.

INDEX

Your Colors At Home

If you would like a set of your colors in your season in a convenient purse-size fan deck of more than 200 colors for only $15, send in the coupon below.

☐ YES! Please send me my season's over 200 colors based on the book **"YOUR COLORS AT HOME"** in a convenient purse-sized fan deck.

I am a ☐ Winter ☐ Summer
☐ Spring ☐ Autumn

☐ Or, send all four seasonal palettes for $50 and save $10.

☐ My check for $_____ is enclosed, made out to Acropolis Books Ltd.

☐ Or charge to my VISA, MC, AMEX Credit Card
No. _____ Exp. Date _____.

NAME _____
ADDRESS _____
CITY _____ STATE _____ ZIP_____

MAIL TO: Lauren Smith
Acropolis Books Ltd.
2400 17th St., N.W.
Washington, D.C. 20009

(Please allow three to six weeks for delivery.)